L**O**ST

IN THE ANTARCTIC

by TOD OLSON

LOST IN THE PACIFIC, 1942

LOST IN OUTER SPACE

LOST IN THE AMAZON

LOST IN THE ANTARCTIC

L✺ST
IN THE ANTARCTIC

THE DOOMED VOYAGE of the ENDURANCE

TOD OLSON

Scholastic Inc.

Photos ©: vi and throughout: Daryl Balfour/Getty Images; viii-ix: Scott Polar Research Institute, University of Cambridge/Getty Images; 2: Royal Geographical Society/Getty Images; 5: Scott Polar Research Institute, University of Cambridge/Getty Images; 10: Christie's Images/Bridgeman Images; 16-17: Scholastic, Inc.; 19: Royal Geographical Society/Getty Images; 21: National Library of Australia; 25: Scott Polar Research Institute, University of Cambridge, with permission; 29, 31, 37, 40, 42: Scott Polar Research Institute, University of Cambridge/Getty Images; 47: Royal Geographical Society/ Getty Images; 52: Scott Polar Research Institute, University of Cambridge/Getty Images; 56: Royal Geographical Society/Getty Images; 61, 64, 70, 74: Scott Polar Research Institute, University of Cambridge/Getty Images; 77: Scott Polar Research Institute, University of Cambridge, with permission; 80-81: Scholastic, Inc.; 84-85: Hulton Archive/Getty Images; 89: Scott Polar Research Institute, University of Cambridge/Getty Images; 94, 98, 106, 108: Royal Geographical Society/Getty Images; 116-117: Daryl Balfour/Getty Images; 124: Royal Geographical Society/Getty Images; 126: Scott Polar Research Institute, University of Cambridge, with permission; 131: Scholastic, Inc.; 133: Scott Polar Research Institute, University of Cambridge, with permission; 137: Royal Geographical Society/Getty Images; 142: Anthony Pierce/Alamy Stock Photo; 148: Royal Geographical Society/Getty Images; 152: Stephen Venables; 155, 163, 170: Royal Geographical Society/Getty Images; 172, 179: Scott Polar Research Institute, University of Cambridge/Getty Images.

Illustrations by: cover and throughout, Shane Rebenschied; 16, 80, 131 maps Jim McMahon

Copyright © 2019 by Tod Olson

Library of Congress Cataloging-in-Publication Data available

ISBN 978-1-338-20734-7

10 9 8 7 6 5 4 3   19 20 21 22 23

Printed in the U.S.A.   23
First edition, January 2019

Book design by Christopher Stengel

For Jill,
who can never get enough ice and snow

TABLE OF CONTENTS

CAST OF CHARACTERS

THE CREW OF THE ENDURANCE

Top row: Stoker Ernest Holness and seaman William Bakewell
Second row: Carpenter Harry McNish, physicist Reginald James, first mate
Frank Wild, Captain Frank Worsley, stoker William Stephenson, navigator Huberht
Hudson, seaman Walter How, cook Charles Green
Third row: Third officer Alf Cheetham, second officer Tom Crean, meteorologist
Leonard Hussey, first officer Lionel Greenstreet, "the Boss" Ernest Shackleton,
Sir Daniel Gooch (returned early to England), engineer Louis Rickinson,
photographer Frank Hurley
Front row: Biologist Robert Clark, geologist James Wordie, doctor Alexander
Macklin, artist George Marston, doctor James McIlroy (five sailors and the
storekeeper Thomas Orde-Lees not pictured)

WEDDELL SEA, ANTARCTICA

October 26, 1915

The ship didn't stand a chance, and Frank Hurley knew it. He'd been in the engine room with the carpenter, trying desperately to keep the water out. They had walled off the leak, where the sternpost and rudder had been wrenched out of place.

It was hard to imagine how it had happened. The sternpost was a giant pillar of hardwood embedded in a 144-foot ship, and the ice had ripped it loose like an angry kid abusing a toy boat. That was the power this frozen land had over them.

Caulking the wall was miserable, frigid work for Hurley and the carpenter. Ice water soaked their boots. Cold air gnawed their fingers raw.

They were patching seams when Hurley heard the pressure hit again—a fierce grinding sound just outside the hull. On the other side of those planks, the ship

The *Endurance*, trapped in a sea of ice 1,000 miles wide.

stood trapped in a vast frozen sea. Slabs of ice the size of small buildings held her in a vise, and now the grip was tightening. The sidewalls groaned and creaked. The noise tore through the cramped compartment. Any minute, it seemed, the boards would splinter, and the ship that had sheltered them for more than a year would finally give up the fight.

The *Endurance* was being squeezed to death around them.

Hurley raced up on deck and took in the scene. The sled dogs, trapped in their kennels, sent out a chorus of howls. The men moved quietly by contrast. They disappeared into the hold and came out with crates rescued from the rising water below. There was canned meat and powdered milk, flour and sugar, rice and barley—all of it ready to be lowered to the ice at a moment's notice.

Tents and sleeping bags had piled up in a corner of the deck—just a few yards of flimsy canvas, reindeer hide, and wool. If the ship gave in, the crew would have nothing else to shelter them from the worst weather on Earth. Today, the sky was blindingly clear, but the temperature hadn't made it above zero degrees Fahrenheit.

Stretching to the horizon around Hurley and the men and the ship was the new home that awaited them: 1 million square miles of ice—an entire sea, frozen almost solid. Beyond it lay Antarctica, a continent bigger than the United States and Mexico combined, also covered in ice and completely uninhabited.

As the expedition's official photographer, Hurley had spent a year capturing the strange, stark beauty of this world. Now, he and 27 other men were about to be dropped into it with no guarantee they would ever get out.

———◆———

One man stood mostly still, watching the commotion from the raised deck in the stern. The crew referred to him as Sir Ernest in writing. In person they called him "the Boss." He had broad shoulders and a compact frame, blunt features and a square jaw. He looked like he was built for this kind of venture—leaving every known thing behind to risk his life in a frozen wilderness.

Ernest Shackleton had been to the Antarctic twice already. Twice he had almost died there. Now, his third expedition hovered on the brink of disaster.

The expedition had left England more than a year ago, in August 1914. The goal was to cross the Antarctic continent by dogsled—1,800 miles in a land where temperatures can drop to −80 degrees at night. It was an ambitious idea. *Crazy* was another word used to describe it.

Just getting to the Antarctic coast to start the overland journey was a near impossible feat. Shackleton had decided

The Boss, Ernest Shackleton.

to sail south from South America and push deep into the Weddell Sea, headed for a landing point at Vahsel Bay. That meant navigating a body of water roughly 1,000 miles across, most of it frozen into sheets of ever-shifting ice that could crush the ship into splinters—"the pack," as it was called.

The *Endurance* had to make its way with a mix of finesse and brute force. Sometimes she nosed her way through open waterways. Sometimes she made her own openings by ramming the ice head-on until it split down the middle.

In January 1915, both strategies had failed. The pack froze around them, and the ship had nowhere to go. It was now October, and the ice still held her prisoner.

The Boss knew how close they had come to their goal. Vahsel Bay had been a day's sail away when the ice grabbed them for good. If only the current and the wind had opened a clear lane 60 miles farther. Shackleton and five companions would right now be trekking across Antarctica—an epic journey to the bottom of the world.

Standing on the deck with the *Endurance* groaning under his feet, Shackleton still had hope. If the ship held out long enough, the pack would break up. They could sail into open water. They might even be able to resupply in South America and make another run at Vahsel Bay before the sea froze solid again.

But right now, some combination of current and wind was squeezing the pack together, and the *Endurance* was caught in the middle. Where the pressure built to a breaking point, the ice buckled into giant ridges. Slabs 5 feet thick and 20 feet tall sprouted into long, jagged tents. To Shackleton it seemed like a mighty giant, buried under the ice, was writhing to break free. He'd been watching all day while a ridge on the starboard side slowly rumbled closer to the ship.

At around 6 p.m., the pressure began to close a crack that had opened behind the *Endurance*. Two giant sheets of ice—known as floes—ground together. They lifted the stern and jerked the entire ship forward in a series of shocks—one, then another, then another. The force wedged her bow into a floe 5 feet thick, squeezing her from end to end.

The deck under Shackleton's feet twisted and bent. Gaps inches wide opened between the planks. He could actually see the sidewalls bend under the strain like an archer's bow. If the front end of the *Endurance* didn't slip above the floe that held it fast, the ship wouldn't last the night.

Shackleton gave the order to lower the lifeboats to the ice. The three 20-foot boats could soon be the only seaworthy vessels they had.

Then, sometime after 8 p.m., the pressure suddenly gave up its hold on the ship. The aching timbers settled back into place. The terrible creaks and groans faded. There was only the steady *clickety-clack* of the pumps, laboring to stay ahead of the leaks. The crew would have to man the pumps in shifts all through the night. But maybe—just maybe—the worst of the damage had been done.

When Frank Hurley went below for the night, he took out his diary and wrote, "All hope is not given up yet for saving the ship."

But for many of the men, a strange memory lingered as they lay in their bunks. In the evening, just as the pressure reached its height, eight emperor penguins had hopped up from a crack in the ice. They waddled in their stiff, strangely human way toward the ship. The birds lined up in formation as if to give a formal address to the intruder in their land. For a few seconds, they chattered the way they often did—a range of calls between a pigeon's coo and a crow's shrill caw. Then they threw back their heads and let out an eerie, wailing fugue.

The men had seen plenty of penguins during the last ten months, but they had never heard a sound like this. To the ship's captain, Frank Worsley, it seemed the creatures were singing a funeral dirge for the *Endurance*.

Thomas McLeod, one of the older seamen, watched the ghostly concert from the deck. He turned to the man next to him. "Do you hear that?" he said in his Scottish brogue. "We'll none of us get back to our homes again."

CHAPTER 1

THE LAST GREAT JOURNEY

Early in 1914, months before the *Endurance* took 28 men 9,000 miles from home, a new sign went up at 4 New Burlington Street in London. It read: IMPERIAL TRANS-ANTARCTIC EXPEDITION. The sign was 3 feet tall and hung at eye level. It stood out in the fashionable neighborhood of jewelry stores and clothing shops. To the wealthy men and women who lived nearby, it may have seemed like a romantic call to adventure.

To Ernest Shackleton it was the business at hand. He didn't like to be confined to an office, but he needed to hire a crew and he had to interview them all somewhere. He had announced the journey in the newspapers—an invitation to spend the next couple of years in the coldest, least populated place on Earth.

Five thousand people responded.

Some of the applicants were lifetime sailors who couldn't

The offices of the Imperial Trans-Antarctic Expedition, open for business.

stand more than a year at a time on dry land. Some were scientists, hoping for a chance to study the strange conditions in a frozen land. Others were drawn by the promise of adventure, of a ripping good tale to tell their kids and grandkids. Still others simply wanted a seaman's job that would pay them decent money for a couple of years.

Shackleton worked closely with his longtime friend and second-in-command, Frank Wild. Together they divided the applications into piles: "Mad," "Hopeless," and "Possible." It was the Possibles who filed through the office on New Burlington Street in the spring of 1914. Rarely did the interviews last longer than five minutes.

When Leonard Hussey walked in the door and sat down, Shackleton was too restless to sit with him. Instead, he paced the floor and talked nonstop. As a meteorologist, Hussey was applying for one of the more important jobs the expedition had to offer. He would attempt to predict the brutal weather on the journey. But his experience hadn't exactly prepared him for blizzards and sub-zero temperatures. He'd spent the last year working in the African desert.

Shackleton didn't seem to care where Hussey had been or what his qualifications were. He walked around for a few minutes, talking more than listening. Finally, he decided he liked Hussey's sense of humor. "Yes, I like you," he declared. "I'll take you."

Reginald James had an equally baffling experience. James applied to be the expedition's physicist, but Shackleton didn't ask a thing about science. He wanted to know instead if James could sing. Not opera, he said, "but I suppose you can shout a bit with the boys?"

Shackleton also asked if James had good circulation. James told him that one of his fingers tended to go numb in the cold. In response, Shackleton asked how attached to that finger James was. Would he mind losing it to frostbite on the way across Antarctica?

———◆———

To the scientists, the interview process may have seemed like a joke. But Antarctica had taken a lot more than fingers from the humans who dared to travel there. And few people knew more about the dangers than Ernest Shackleton.

When Shackleton was in his twenties, Antarctica was one of the last great mysterious places on Earth. European soldiers and explorers had marched across nearly every other part of the globe. But here was a continent bigger than Europe, and barely anyone had set foot on its shores.

For thousands of years, people had only guessed at its existence. The ancient Greeks knew there was land near the North Pole, and they decided there had to be a continent in the south to balance out the globe. This legendary place became known as *Terra Australis,* or South Land. In the 1500s, geographers put *Terra Australis* on their maps, even though no one knew for sure it was there. Some people even imagined a land full of rivers, parrots, and "good, honest" people.

The British explorer James Cook finally sailed below the Antarctic Circle in 1773 and put an end to the Great South Land fantasy. Dodging through a maze of icebergs—which he called "ice islands"—he made it farther south than anyone had ever gone.

No one would get farther, Cook predicted. In his opinion, there was no reason to try. All he had seen was a "horrid" region of blizzards and soupy fog. The entire place was "doomed by Nature never to feel the warmth of the sun's rays, but to lie for ever buried under everlasting snow and ice."

Shackleton first ventured into the snow and ice in 1901. By that time, Antarctica had been discovered and named. But no one had gotten near the South Pole.

A British navy officer named Robert Scott made the first serious attempt. In August 1901, he left England on the ship *Discovery* with Shackleton as his third officer. After wintering in Antarctica, Shackleton, Scott, and the scientist Edward Wilson set off toward the Pole in November 1902 with 19 dogs and five sleds packed with supplies. None of the men had much experience skiing or handling dogs. Three months later they stumbled back to their ship, frostbitten and snow-blind. Shackleton was spitting blood and nearly dead from the nutritional disease scurvy.

But he couldn't wait to try again.

In 1908 he went back, as leader of an expedition. This time he almost reached the Pole. He set out from the coast with three men, including his friend Frank Wild. They bumbled their way south with four ponies to pull supplies. When the ponies sunk to their bellies in the snow and had to be put down, the men harnessed themselves to the sleds and trudged on. After 10 weeks of misery, they made it to within 100 miles of the Pole, farther south than anyone had gone before. They nearly starved to death on the way back.

At one point, while packing sleds for another brutal day, Wild looked like he wouldn't last much longer. Shackleton handed over his biscuit ration for the day and insisted Wild take it. "All the money that was ever minted would not have bought that biscuit," Wild wrote in his diary, "and the remembrance of that sacrifice will never leave me."

Shackleton came back to England a hero. He spent the next couple of years touring Europe, giving lectures about his voyage. He dined with dukes and lords. He met the tsar of Russia; the prime minister of Canada; and the American president, William Howard Taft.

By 1912, he was sick of it all and scheming to get back to Antarctica. But while Shackleton had been touring, the Norwegian explorer Roald Amundsen had made it to the Pole. And Robert Scott had frozen to death trying to beat Amundsen there.

While the British were still mourning the loss of Scott, Shackleton announced an even bigger, more audacious plan. "We have been beaten at the conquest of the North Pole and beaten at the conquest of the South Pole," Shackleton wrote. "There now remains the most striking journey of all—the crossing of the Continent."

To do it he would take the *Endurance* through the Weddell Sea to Vahsel Bay. From there he would lead a sledding party of six men 800 miles overland to the South Pole. A second ship, the *Aurora*, would sail into the Ross Sea on the other side of the continent. The *Aurora* would send a sledding party toward the Pole to stash supplies along the second half of Shackleton's journey. If all went well, Shackleton and his team would reach the Pole and trek another 800 miles to the Ross Sea, well supplied along the way.

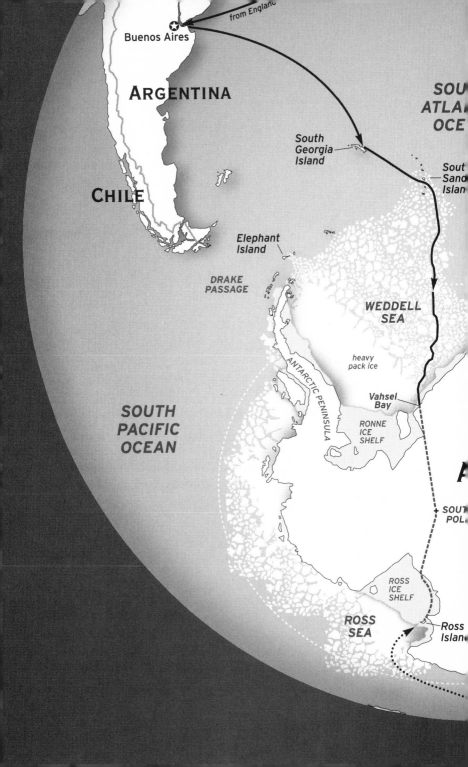

THE IMPERIAL TRANS-ANTARCTIC EXPEDITION
1914–1917

← Route of *Endurance*

---- Planned route across Antarctica

◄···· Route of *Aurora*

0   500
MILES

TCIC CIRCLE

ARCTICA

SOUTH INDIAN OCEAN

TASMANIA

To Shackleton, it was "the last great Polar journey that can be made."

Not everyone was convinced. Admiral Winston Churchill, for one, thought Shackleton's plan was a colossal waste of time and resources. "Enough life and money has been spent on this sterile quest," he wrote. "The Pole has already been discovered. What is the use of another expedition?"

Churchill was in charge of the British navy, and for some years, he'd been locked in a dangerous arms race with the Germans. Warships, tanks, cannons, rifles, and ammunition piled up on both sides. It wouldn't be long before all the life and money Britain had to offer was needed for a struggle far greater than a trip across Antarctica.

On July 14, 1914, a cargo ship chugged up the river Thames into London with a precious but unruly shipment. The ship steamed into the West India Docks. Eventually, about 70 dogs—big, shaggy, and loud—clambered onto the pier, straining at their leashes.

These were not purebreds bound for a dog show. They were mangy, powerful mongrels. To Frank Wild, they looked like a mix of "wolf and any kind of big dog." To the men who were determined to cross Antarctica, they could mean the difference between life and death.

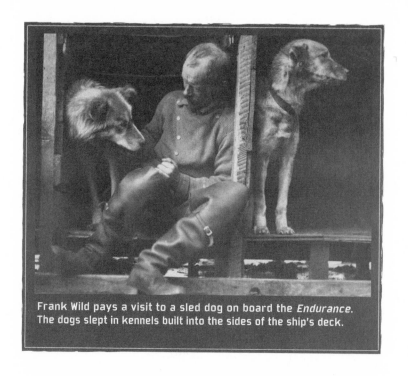

Frank Wild pays a visit to a sled dog on board the *Endurance*. The dogs slept in kennels built into the sides of the ship's deck.

The dogs would provide the muscle for Shackleton's expedition. They would haul sleds packed with food supplies across the snow and ice. Near the end of the journey, after spending all the strength they had on their job, they might themselves become food for a party of starving men. That was the harsh reality of Antarctic exploration.

At the West India Docks, amidst a forest of masts, stood the ship that would carry the dogs and their human companions into the Antarctic. She was called the *Endurance*, and she was built for the task. Planks of oak and fir thicker than telephone poles made up her hull. Her bow was sheathed in greenheart, a wood denser than many others on Earth. Every inch of her had been made with one purpose in mind—to withstand the ice. In case that wasn't enough, in her rigging hung three 20-foot lifeboats, the *James Caird*, the *Dudley Docker*, and the *Stancomb Wills*.

The *Endurance* was packed to the gunwales with supplies. Crates of food filled the dark storeroom. There were dense, high-calorie rations for the sledding journey; tubs of basics like flour and sugar; luxuries like turtle soup, canned herring, figs, dates, and jam. To keep the crew entertained, Shackleton's cabin had a library full of novels, accounts of polar expeditions, and volumes of the *Encyclopedia Britannica*.

Sharing space with the books and the food would be the men who had made it through the interviews on New Burlington Street. Aside from Shackleton, Wild, and Captain Worsley, there were three officers and a navigator. A biologist, a geologist, and two doctors joined the scientific staff. Reginald James had decided to risk his finger in the name of science. Leonard Hussey was about to go from 100-degree days in the desert to a place where temperatures can drop below −100 degrees.

The carpenter, Harry McNish, would have two engineers to help him fix anything that broke down. The

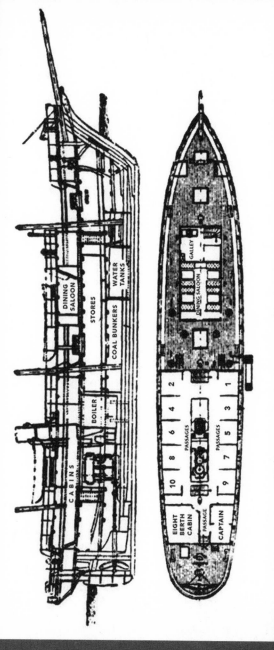

The polar ship *Endurance*, home to 27 men and more than 50 dogs for months to come.

storekeeper, Thomas Orde-Lees, would be in charge of the food supplies. A cook named Charles Green had the thankless task of keeping 28 hungry sailors fed from a cramped ship's galley.

Shackleton had also picked eight seamen to hoist sails, shovel coal into the steam boiler, and do whatever else it took to keep the ship running. Only one of the men had been to the Antarctic before.

Rounding out the crew were two artists whose skills seemed to have little to do with polar exploration. George Marston, a slow-moving but likeable man, brought a supply of paints and sketchbooks. Frank Hurley, who was still in his native Australia, would meet the *Endurance* in Argentina with crates of bulky camera equipment.

Shackleton was counting on Marston and Hurley to supply the images for a film, a lecture tour, and a book when the men got home. At sea or on the ice Shackleton was a great leader and organizer. But he was terrible at managing money. Between expeditions, he always had a get-rich-quick scheme brewing: gold in Hungary, timber in Mexico, buried pirate treasure in the South Pacific. Each scheme was a bigger failure than the last. He often struggled to support his wife, Emily, and their three children.

To pay for the *Endurance*, supplies, and salaries, Shackleton had run up a debt of nearly $4 million in today's money. He could only hope that upon his return, paying customers would be waiting by the thousands to hear about his adventures at the bottom of the world.

———◆———

On August 1, the *Endurance* eased out of its London dock and headed for the coast to start its journey. The next day, 300 miles to the east, tens of thousands of German soldiers stormed into the tiny country of Luxembourg, preparing to invade France. The *Endurance* docked at Margate, looking out on the French coast across the English Channel. Shackleton went ashore to find that the British army was mobilizing. In two days England would declare war on Germany to defend her French ally. Within a week, the First World War would engulf all of Europe.

Shackleton returned to the ship and called everyone together on deck. The months of preparations—of planning and raising money and hiring a crew—looked like they were about to be scrapped. He told the men they were free to join up and fight. Then he sent a message to Churchill offering the ship and the men to the navy.

"If not required," he went on, "I propose continuing voyage forthwith as any delay would prevent expedition getting through pack ice this year."

Churchill sent a one-word reply: "Proceed."

CHAPTER 2
SOUTHBOUND

I t took the *Endurance* two months to cross the Atlantic, and the storekeeper Thomas Orde-Lees did not enjoy the trip.

Sailing out of Plymouth, England, signs of war were everywhere. Battleships steamed in and out of the harbor. Searchlights swept the water at night. Two days before the *Endurance* sailed, a British cruiser hit a German mine in the English Channel and 150 men went down with the ship.

For Lees, that wasn't the half of it. He spent the first week on the Atlantic seasick and barely able to choke down a bowl of soup. When he finally felt up to eating, he didn't like the company. The seamen drank and swore too much for his tastes.

The second week out, Lees forced himself to eat with the barbarians. "I think it is a good thing to try and

Lees on deck. He was nervous about the expedition and almost deserted the ship before it left England.

accommodate oneself to ideas and ways less refined than one's own," he explained to his diary that night.

But when he sat down with the ship's carpenter, he couldn't stand the man's table manners. McNish made annoying sucking sounds, picked his teeth with a match, and spit out the window. Lees was disgusted. The carpenter, he complained, was a "perfect pig in every way."

As if eating with the sailors weren't enough of an indignity, Lees had to work with them too. On a Shackleton expedition, officers and scientists were expected to help run the ship, and Lees whined about having to pull ropes and scrub the decks with the sailors. The ropes were dirty and made his hands sore, he said.

Yet for all Lees's haughtiness, he was right about one thing: The sailors were out of control on the way across the Atlantic. During a stopover on the island of Madeira, four of the men got into a bar fight. One ended up with his scalp sliced open by a sword. Another had his face smashed with a flowerpot.

When the ship finally arrived in Buenos Aires, Argentina, two men went off to get drunk and didn't come back for a week. Shackleton was traveling separately to Buenos Aires, and Lees thought Captain Worsley was too easygoing to keep everyone in line. "It will all be put right when Sir Ernest arrives, thank goodness," Lees wrote.

The *Endurance* headed south from Buenos Aires on October 26, with everything put right for now. The ship was stuffed with fresh supplies. Shackleton had fired the two men who went missing for a week. In their place he hired an American seaman named William Bakewell. Bakewell had turned up at the docks with Perce Blackborow, his 19-year-old friend. Blackborow desperately wanted to sail with the *Endurance*. But he was inexperienced, and Worsley decided they had enough hands to run the ship.

When the *Endurance* steamed out to sea, a small, mostly British crowd gathered to see them off. They waved handkerchiefs, and the crew waved back. The dogs howled while a band played the British anthem, "God Save the King."

There would be one more stop—a whaling station at the last populated place in the frozen south, the isolated island of South Georgia. They would anchor there for a while, stock up on coal and food, and learn from the whalers about the ice conditions in the Weddell Sea. But to everyone on board, it felt like they were finally on their way. The men started singing sea chanties while they set the sails.

For Shackleton it was a relief to leave all the preparations and the money-grubbing behind. He knew how to charm people, but he was happiest where human beings were scarce. The lecturing and the constant money worries had been a chore since he'd come back in 1909. "All the troubles of the South are nothing to day after day of business," he had written to a friend in the middle of it all.

Ahead there would be frostbite and hunger to worry about. But physical hardship was simple—it demanded only courage and a willingness to suffer. "All the strain is finished and there now comes the actual work itself," he wrote in his diary. "The fight will be good."

———◆———

The first challenge came quickly—at 4 p.m. the next day. They were well out to sea when Ernest Holness, one of the stokers, finished his turn tending the ship's coal-burning engines and went to his locker. His clothes hung inside just as he'd left them. But on the floor he found a surprising addition to the wardrobe. A strange pair of boots stuck out from under his oilskin coveralls. In them stood Bakewell's young friend, Perce Blackborow.

A few minutes later Blackborow was presented to Shackleton. The stowaway had been cramped in a locker for a day and a half with nothing but scraps of food to eat. He tried to stand at attention, but Shackleton ordered him to sit.

Blackborow with McNish's cat, Mrs. Chippy.

Blackborow could only hope the Boss wouldn't leave him in South Georgia with no way to get home. Shackleton was hard to predict, after all. All his good cheer could turn to anger in an instant.

Shackleton stared Blackborow down and launched into a tirade. Finally, the Boss leaned close to Blackborow and said, "Do you know that on these expeditions we often get hungry, and if there is a stowaway available he is the first to be eaten?"

Blackborow was either a brave man or Shackleton had a hint of a smirk on his face, because the stowaway looked at the Boss and said, "They'd get a lot more meat off you, sir."

A moment passed. Shackleton, who appreciated a sense of humor, turned to his second-in-command, Wild. "Take him to the bo'sun," he said. "Introduce him to the cook first."

For better or worse, Blackborow was on his way to Antarctica with a job as the cook's helper.

———◆———

Nine days later the *Endurance* steamed into Grytviken Whaling Station on South Georgia. As they made their way into the harbor, the smell was enough to take anyone's appetite away. Several rotting whale carcasses bobbed in the water 200 yards off the wharf. Four more clogged a slip between two piers. Men stood on the piers with 10-foot-long lances, slicing thick slabs of blubber off the dead giants.

The shore was a vast graveyard—except someone had forgotten to bury the corpses. Hurley counted at least 100 whale skulls, some as long as the 20-foot lifeboats on board the *Endurance*.

If the "Great South Land," had anything of benefit to humans, this was it. For more than a century, whales in all the world's oceans had been hunted ruthlessly for profit. Oil from their blubber was burned in lamps, boiled into soap, and congealed into margarine.

A mammoth blue whale carcass at Grytviken, waiting to have the blubber stripped from its skeleton, a process known as flensing.

By the early 1900s, the whaleships had done their job too well. Whales were few and far between in northern waters. But in the southern summer they gathered around Antarctica by the thousands to feed on swarms of tiny crustaceans called krill.

From September to March, the Antarctic teemed with fin whales, majestic humpbacks, and blue whales the size of buses. They were the biggest mammals on Earth, too big for predators in the water. But their size made them slow and easy prey for the most ingenious predator of all—humankind.

The year before the *Endurance* arrived, Antarctic hunters had slaughtered nearly 10,000 whales. South Georgia alone was churning out 200,000 barrels of oil a year.

Hurley was disgusted by the whalers but fascinated by the process. He toured the factory where they boiled the blubber into oil. He learned about the exploding harpoons that scrambled a whale's innards. He discovered the practice of inflating whale carcasses with air so they wouldn't sink while they were towed home.

On the third night in South Georgia, the Norwegian manager of the whaling station invited the officers of the *Endurance* to dinner. Hurley went separately from the rest. A couple of sailors rowed him ashore and returned to the ship.

The photographer picked his way through the whale graveyard by the light of an oil lamp. Eventually, he found his way blocked by a fresh corpse. The head lay too close to the water to climb around. A pile of steaming intestines cut off the path around the tail. Hurley decided to brave a set of ladders bridging the way up and over the corpse. Halfway across he lost his balance and went tumbling into the dark, clammy, wide-open carcass of the whale.

Hurley tried a few times to scramble out, but traction was lacking. Finally, he gave up, swallowed his pride, and yelled for help. With the stench of whale innards still clinging to his clothes, he would later conclude, "It is impossible to view this trade with other than loathing."

———◆———

Cleaned up as best he could manage, Hurley joined Shackleton, Captain Worsley, and others for dinner at the home of the whaling station manager. Fridjof Jacobsen's home was a welcome relief from the garbage heap outside. The men gathered in a sitting room with singing canaries and a piano. They played billiards and enjoyed an eight-course meal on fine china.

During the evening, the conversation turned to the expedition. Jacobsen confirmed what they had already heard in Buenos Aires. In the Southern hemisphere, where winter runs from June to September, spring was under way. In normal conditions, the pack ice in the Weddell Sea would be breaking up by now. But the winter had been bitterly cold, and it wasn't warming as fast as expected. The ice still extended north of the Weddell into the South Atlantic. It would make for hard sailing if the *Endurance* left now.

Jacobsen, it turned out, had a famous father-in-law who had firsthand experience with the Weddell Sea ice. All the men had heard the story of Carl Larsen's voyage, but they discussed it again over whale steaks and sausage made from whale-fed pigs.

Larsen had captained the ship *Antarctic* into the northwestern edge of the Weddell Sea in January 1903. He was returning to pick up the head of his expedition, the Norwegian geologist Otto Nordenskjöld. Nordenskjöld had been exploring the icy outpost of Snow Hill Island with five other men since February the year before.

The *Antarctic* rammed and prodded through the pack, trying to force its way to Snow Hill. On January 10, the ship began to shudder like a leaf in the wind. The shifting ice wedged itself under the hull with an ear-splitting crash and lifted the *Antarctic* four feet out of the water. That night the ship settled again, but a third of the keel had been torn away. Water gushed through a hole in the stern.

Six pumps chugged like mad to keep up with the leaks. But a month later, the water won. The men abandoned ship and watched while the *Antarctic* went under. "She is breathing her last," wrote the ship's botanist. "Now the water is up to the rail, and bits of ice rush in over her deck. That sound I can never forget, however long I may live."

Larsen and his crew of 20 had to winter on the ice. Three of his men finally reached Nordenskjöld by land at the end of 1903, and the entire party was saved by an Argentine ship. By this time, Nordenskjöld and his two companions had been living on penguin meat for 21 months. They were alive but frostbitten and dazed after two winters in the Antarctic. Nordenskjöld was desperate for the sight of a single blade of grass. The vast expanse of white, pale blue, and brown, he said, radiated "something which resembles the chill of death."

In the comfort of Jacobsen's villa, Shackleton finished off his meal with an expensive cigar. After the night's conversation, he decided to wait a month in South Georgia before setting off. Hopefully, the pack would begin to break up. Then he and Worsley would lead the *Endurance* south, 850 miles deeper into the ice than Carl Larsen's ship had gone when it was crushed beneath the feet of its crew.

CHAPTER 3

RAMMING

O n December 5, the *Endurance* slipped past the rotting
whale carcasses into the South Atlantic. Shackleton
had spent the last few days waiting for a British ship
to arrive with news of the war. Finally, he decided they
couldn't wait any longer. The height of the Antarctic
summer was two weeks away. After that, the days grew
shorter, the weather colder, and the ice thicker.

Riding the swells, the ship looked a mess. Thirty tons
of coal had been heaped on the deck to feed the ship's
steam engines. A ton of whale meat hung from the rigging.
Whale blood dripped onto the kennels below, whipping
the dogs into a frenzy. As soon as the dogs calmed down,
McNish's cat, Mrs. Chippy, pranced the length of the
kennels, tormenting them into another fit.

To the sweet music of six dozen dogs howling, the men
watched the South Georgia coastline fade into the horizon.

The *Endurance* on its way into the Weddell Sea. Dogs outnumbered humans by more than two to one.

Most of them knew it could be a year and a half before they saw another piece of land settled by humans.

One thousand miles to the southeast lay Vahsel Bay, their gateway to a place that barely supports life of any kind. For 30 million years, snow has been falling on Antarctica, compressing with the force of gravity and turning to ice. You could walk the entire continent in midsummer and your feet would hit bare land less than 2 percent of the time. In places, you would have to drill through 2 miles of ice to reach the ground. Below the ice are mountain ranges the size of the Rockies whose peaks never see the light of day.

The weather on this barren ice cap is brutal. At the Pole, the average winter temperature sinks to −75 degrees. Winds whip down off the coastal mountains at 150 miles per hour. The British explorer Apsley Cherry-Garrard was crazy enough to attempt a winter trek on the Antarctic coast in 1911. When a blizzard blew his tent away, he was convinced he would never see home again. "I have never heard or felt or seen a wind like this," he wrote. "I wondered why it did not carry away the Earth."

The weather is so inhospitable that no land mammal spends the entire year in Antarctica. The largest land creature to stay there year round is a 1/4-inch-long insect known as a wingless midge. Even the sea creatures need special defenses to survive. Fish that make it through the winter carry a kind of antifreeze in their blood made of sugar and proteins. Some are so rugged they've been found frozen solid in the ice—and perfectly alive.

———◆———

The *Endurance* hit pack ice on her fifth day out, much sooner than the Boss had hoped. Shackleton thought of the pack as a vast jigsaw puzzle of ice. Most of the pieces are slabs 5 to 6 feet high and covered in snow. Some are as small as barges, others as big as islands. In loose pack, the pieces float apart and press together again. In the lanes between the slabs, known as leads, the water freezes into thin, brittle "young ice." When the pack closes, the pieces squeeze together and the sea becomes land as far as the eye can see.

Everyone knew what the ice could do to a ship. But it didn't seem to bother Worsley. "The Skipper," as the crew called him, guided the *Endurance* through the obstacle course as though it were the most fun a human being could have on Earth. Standing high in the bow, he scanned the pack for leads. McNish had built him an 8-foot-tall arrow that swiveled in an arc. Worsley used it to tell the helmsman, 140 feet away in the stern, which way to steer.

Most of the time, the ship crunched and ground its way through young ice. When an island-sized floe blocked their path, Worsley had two choices. He could navigate around the chunk. But if the ice measured less than 3 feet thick, he chose the option he obviously preferred: Ram the floe till it split down the middle.

When Worsley gave the signal, the stoker built up steam in the engine and slammed full speed into the ice. The bow of the *Endurance*, 4 feet thick and strong as iron, lifted like it was about to lead the ship out of the water onto the floe. Then it settled, carving a bow-shaped notch into

Entering pack ice on December 9, 1914.

the ice. At Worsley's urging they reversed the engines, backed up, and rammed again. This time, if they were lucky, a crack would open and spread with a croaking echo into the distance. With a few more bone-crunching impacts, the floe finally split like an island torn apart by an earthquake.

Worsley stood in the bow through the whole process like a rodeo rider on a bull, the ship bucking under his feet. "It's a splendid sensation," he crowed to his diary. Alexander Macklin, one of the doctors on board, was convinced that the Skipper went out of his way to find hunks of ice to smash. "Worsley specialized in ramming," he said.

It might have been great fun to Worsley, but Lees was not impressed. The storekeeper sat below, trying to write in his diary. Every time the ship hit a slab of ice, it jerked the book from under his pen. The grinding outside the walls sounded like thunder. He was sure the hull was about to cave in.

———◆———

They fought their way south, sometimes skirting the ice and sometimes blasting their way through. In open water, the *Endurance* could cover 200 miles a day. In the pack, she made 33 miles one day, 53 the next, 18 after that. The next day the ship lost 6 miles, drifting backward with the ice.

On December 18, they plowed through seas that looked to Lees like "one great solid desert snowfield." He worried they were burning through their coal supply trying to make headway. The following day they gave up, anchored the ship to a floe, and drifted with the ice.

The men decided to make the most of the delay. They were so far south at this point that the sun, at the height of the summer, never set. Even at midnight it hovered just above the horizon, giving off a strange dim glow. In the midnight sun, the crew turned out onto the ice and planted tall poles in the snow for goals. Then they shed their jackets and played soccer, Antarctic style. The scientists and most of the officers made up one team, with Shackleton in goal. But the seamen refused to go easy on the Boss. They finished with a 2–0 victory.

Soccer on the ice, with the *Endurance* standing watch behind.

The *Endurance* got under way again on December 21. They had put 700 miles between themselves and the nearest members of the human species. But they had plenty of companions—a constant escort from the creatures that clawed out a living on the ice. Snow petrels and skuas swooped low over the ship, hoping to snatch a bite of meat. Occasionally a blue whale, half the size of the ship, broke the surface of the water, blasting plumes of spray into the air. Killer whales with their ominous triangular fins prowled the edges of the ice, waiting for a seal to make a wrong move.

Of all the residents of the frozen sea, it was the penguins that provided the best entertainment. They shot out of the water like vaulters from an underwater trampoline. Landing with a *thud* on their bellies, they skidded to a stop on the ice.

Sometimes the little Adélie penguins followed the ship from a nearby floe, squawking at the crew. That gave the men a chance to have a little fun with the biologist, Robert Clark, who rarely cracked a smile. They decided the penguins all knew Clark, because whenever the biologist was at the wheel the birds hustled along, screaming "Clark! Clark!" No matter how many times the men told him to answer the penguins, Clark refused to play along.

For the penguins and the seals, however, the fun and games often stopped in a brutal instant. The men had planned to add to their food supply as they traveled. Usually the hunt was no contest. The penguins knew to avoid sea leopards and killer whales. But most of them had never seen a human being before. They simply stood on the ice and waited for the men to club them to death.

———◆———

Sometimes, the world around the *Endurance* was so strange and beautiful the men could only pause and stare. Worsley felt like they were seeing things no human had ever seen before. Even Lees stopped grumbling to marvel at the scenery.

Icebergs floated like giant sculptures in the water. Some lay stubby and flat. Others rose from the sea like castles in a fantasyland, spires poking at the sky. The waves beat against the sides of the taller bergs, and spray shot to the top of the cliffs. In places, the water carved hollow caverns into the base of the ice with a great booming sound.

The scenery, to Hurley, was like whale meat to the dogs. He was a born adventurer who ran away from home at 14. Now, on that rare sunny day when the light gleamed off the ice in just the right way, he would do anything to capture it on film. He'd gather his cameras, climb into the rigging, and edge out onto an icy spar. He perched like a bird, oblivious to the danger and the cold. When the light and the angle were just right, he took his pictures. Worsley could hear him from down below cursing into the wind in triumph when he thought he'd gotten the perfect shot.

———◆———

As the sea ice grew thicker and more treacherous, Shackleton tried to keep the men in a good mood. He encouraged the sightseeing and the penguin jokes and the soccer in the snow. Twice before, he'd been close to death and hundreds of miles from safety, and he knew that morale could make all the difference. Men who wanted to work together survived. Men who bickered and held grudges did not.

Still, progress was slow, and Shackleton felt the strain. By the dawn of the new year they were 480 miles out from South Georgia—less than halfway to Vahsel Bay. During the day, the Boss spent long hours in the crow's nest at the top of the mast. Standing 60 feet above the deck, he scanned the giant ice puzzle, looking for open water. There had to be a path somewhere out there that would take them to Vahsel Bay.

Five weeks out from South Georgia, Lees thought Shackleton looked exhausted. "Sir Ernest looks dead tired," he wrote. "He has been up at night so much lately; and the anxiety of the last few days, to which he never owned, must have pulled him down."

———◆———

On January 10, a sight appeared off the port bow to lift Shackleton's mood—a giant wall of ice, rising 100 feet from the surface of the sea. They had found their first stretch of open water in weeks, and the *Endurance* had made use of it. She made 100 miles in 24 hours, and here for the first time loomed the barrier ice that lined the coast of Antarctica.

All around the continent, masses of ice called glaciers crawl from the high mountains down toward the sea. (For a glacier, 2 inches an hour is a fast pace.) At the coast, these ice giants form the floating cliffs known as barrier ice that the crew now gawked at from the deck.

They sailed southwest along the barrier, knowing now that Vahsel Bay lay within reach. Just before midnight on January 15, the *Endurance* pulled into a quiet bay, protected to the south by a 500-foot-high glacier. Even at midnight, the summer sun cast a dim glow around the bay. At the shore, the ice made a perfect landing spot, just 3 feet above the water. Shackleton named the inlet Glacier Bay.

The Boss conferred with his officers. Worsley thought they should land the shore party while they had the chance and start the overland trek from there. But they were still about 200 miles north of Vahsel Bay. That would add two weeks to the journey, and Shackleton didn't want to risk it. After all, they had clear seas to the south. They were in the middle of their best run in weeks.

Barrier ice looms off the ship's bow on January 10—the rugged edge of a continent buried in ice.

At noon, three days later, Worsley calculated their position. Vahsel Bay lay just 104 miles away. One more stretch of open water and there would be congratulations to go around. The Boss, no doubt, would break out the fine food and drink. The Weddell Sea had given them all they could handle, but they had fought their way through.

Lees spent the day sorting through supplies, separating the crates marked "ship" from the crates marked "shore." When he turned in that night at 9 p.m., he wrote, "Spirits are high all round as we are all eagerly looking forward to the change which landing will mean."

CHAPTER 4

FAST IN THE ICE

On January 19, the morning after Lees started getting ready to land, the entire crew woke to a grim sight. The ice had closed tight against the sides of the ship. Worsley climbed to the crow's nest, hoping to find a way out. "No water in sight from deck," he wrote that night, "very little from masthead & dull gloomy pall over the sky since noon."

The carpenter, McNish, who wasn't one to waste words, started keeping track of their progress in his diary.

"Thursday 21st . . . we are still fast in the ice . . ."

"Friday 22nd still in the same predicament with no signs of any change . . ."

"Saturday 23rd still fast . . ."

"Sunday 24th still fast & no signs of any opening pressure . . ."

"Monday 25th still fast . . ."

That's not to say the *Endurance* wasn't moving. The pack ice in the Weddell Sea swirls clockwise like a giant pinwheel, 1,000 miles across. The ship and her 28 human occupants had become part of the pack, and they drifted with it to the southwest. By February 1, they could almost see their goal. Vahsel Bay was just 59 miles away.

It might as well have been halfway around the Earth. The ice between the ship and the coast was uneven and riddled with cracks. One man on skis would be hard-pressed to make the trip without plunging into 30-degree water. Hauling tons of supplies by sled was out of the question.

———◆———

No one was willing to admit they were stuck for good. But their prospects looked bad. They needed warm temperatures and a stiff south wind to break up the pack. Instead, the wind died completely, and the temperature dropped below zero. By the second week, they ran out of seal meat, and Lees started hoarding the canned food. "I grudge every tin of meat now," he wrote.

With no sailing to keep them occupied, the men started to get restless. On Saturday nights, Shackleton let the crew gather in the wardroom, sing, and drink a toast to "sweethearts and wives." The second Saturday in the ice,

McNish drank more than his share and got into a fight in the forecastle.

A few days later, Lees and McNish were battling over Lees's beloved storeroom. McNish thought Lees spent all his time fussing around and never did any useful work. So as soon as Lees got everything organized just right, McNish would come looking for something and leave the room a mess. "He has an exceptionally offensive manner and it is very hard to be patient with him," Lees huffed.

Shackleton had picked crew members he thought would get along with each other. But McNish was the one man he didn't trust.

Every day, while the crew tried to keep busy, Shackleton and Worsley climbed the mast to scan for open leads. The light and the endless expanse of white often played tricks on their eyes. Clouds looked like icebergs and icebergs dangled upside down from the sky. Worst of all, if the angle of light was just right, a streak of open water appeared in the distance. If they squinted long enough they realized it was just an illusion.

On February 5 the ice shifted and the ship settled into open water with a sharp jolt. Everyone rushed on deck to see if they'd been liberated, but they were stuck in a small pool, surrounded by ice. That night, the water around them froze solid again.

On Valentine's Day, Shackleton called all hands together. The winds had been blowing again from the southwest. The pack seemed to be loosening. From the masthead, open water appeared a third of a mile off—and this time, it wasn't a mirage. They were going to make one final attempt to get free.

The crew climbed onto the floe to battle the ice. Two dozen men hacked away near the bow of the ship with pickaxes, giant ice saws, and 10-foot-tall iron poles. They carved the ice into blocks and hauled them aside. It was exhausting work, but eventually, they gave the *Endurance* 10 feet of open water.

With Lees at the wheel, Worsley rammed a thick, lumpy section of the pack again and again. The men moved ahead and worked on the young ice beyond the lump.

All day they chipped and sawed and hauled with the temperature hovering around 10 degrees. By midnight, the men were soaked and chilled to the bone. They had opened a hole the size of half a tennis court.

By 4 p.m. the next day, a day and a half of labor had moved the ship 200 yards. Between the *Endurance* and the open water lay 400 more yards of 10-foot-thick ice. And the water was freezing up as fast as they could clear it.

Shackleton called off the effort.

Valentine's Day labors: trying to carve out a path to open water.

The order came as no surprise. It would have been hard to find a single person on board who thought they had a chance in the first place. "Puny mortals striving frantically against the mighty forces of nature," Lees wrote. "The laughing stock of the Gods; only a handful of us contending against all that ice."

But gone for the moment were the restlessness and the petty squabbles. "I never saw such unanimous cooperation and intensity of purpose," Lees concluded. And that was probably the point to begin with. Shackleton knew that grumbling started when there was nothing to do. He also knew that in the months ahead, these men were going to need to work together. This was a training session.

That night, the sun dipped below the horizon for the first time in three and a half months. The days would shorten fast. In April or May the sun would vanish for several more long, dark months. Winter was on its way, and the crew of the *Endurance* would spend it trapped in the ice.

On February 24, Shackleton ordered an end to normal ship duties. He put all hands to work storing seal meat and moving supplies out of the cargo hold below. With a little work, the hold, sheltered from the wind and the cold, would become their winter quarters. "Today . . . we practically cease being a ship & become a winter station," Worsley recorded.

For now, they had food. They could melt snow and ice for drinking water. Maybe in a few months the ice would loosen. Maybe the giant rotating pack would carry them far enough north to find open water. Then they could resupply in South America and try to make their way back to Vahsel Bay.

In the meantime the ship would be their only shelter from temperatures cold enough to freeze tears on a man's face. But who could say for sure how long it would survive?

"We will have to wait Gods will to get out," McNish wrote. "Temperature +2."

CHAPTER 5

WINTERING

solated from the world and trapped for the winter, the men felt a gloom settle over the ship. "A wave of depression seemed to come over everybody on board," wrote James Wordie, the geologist. "It was soon noticed that it was best not to get in the Boss's way."

But while the men sensed Shackleton's anxiety, the Boss didn't show it openly. He explained calmly that they would spend the winter in the pack. Then he put the men to work.

The first task was to build winter quarters—and the crew weren't the only ones in need. Worsley spent the first week of March supervising a team of doghouse builders out on the ice. The team sawed blocks of ice from the floe and stacked them into round walls for tiny huts. They used boards or sealskin for the roofs. Then they packed snow on top and poured water over the huts to freeze them into place. By March 5, a ring of icy doghouses surrounded the ship. The sailors called their masterpieces "dogloos."

While the dogloo builders did their work, McNish built a home belowdecks for most of the officers and the scientists. He made cubicles in the empty hold and put bunks in each one. A table occupied the middle of the room. A potbellied stove stood in the corner. The sailors would stay in the forecastle, where they always slept. Shackleton would sleep in his drafty cabin on the deck.

Like kids moving into a cabin at camp, Lees, Hurley, Hussey, and the rest set up their quarters. They gave their cubicles names, and Hurley carved little wooden plaques for each one. Pictures of loved ones went up near the

The *Endurance* with its neighboring village of dogloos.

bunks. The roommates called their primitive hideaway "the Ritz," after the most luxurious hotel in London.

The only thing more important than shelter was food. That became only too clear to the seals and penguins that came to investigate the intruders in their midst. It was Worsley's job to stand on the masthead with a telescope and binoculars, scanning the ice for life. When he saw movement, he called out directions to a party of hunters through a megaphone.

Frank Wild often led the hunting parties, pistol in hand. They went out on skis or by dogsled. If everything went according to plan, Wild dispatched his prey with one shot to the head. But sometimes the hunt turned into a brutal slaughter. Lees and Worsley once wounded a seal but ran out of ammunition before they could kill it. They finished the job by clubbing the maimed animal to death with an oar. According to Worsley, "It was an awful bloody business."

But the men had a feeling that at any moment the hunters could become the hunted. They had seen killer whales stalk seals or penguins under young ice. When the 10,000-pound predators saw their chance they came rocketing up from below, shattering the ice with their heads. If they aimed well, the blow sent their prey tumbling into the water, and the whales put their 4-inch-long teeth to work gathering dinner. "More villainous . . . looking creatures I have never seen," wrote Hurley after watching a couple of killers come up for a look at the *Endurance*.

The men lived in fear that a killer whale might have trouble telling the difference between a seal and a human.

———●———

After dinner on Saturday May 1, the officers of the *Endurance* said good-bye to the light. The next day, the sun disappeared below the horizon. It wouldn't make another appearance for three and a half months. For a week or so, the temperature failed to rise above zero. Some mornings the dogs had to be hacked out of the ice because their body heat melted the snow during the night and the water froze around them.

The Antarctic winter had begun, and the cold wasn't the only thing to fear. Three and a half months without sunlight could make even the hardiest sailor begin to question his sanity. Anyone who doubted that fact had only to listen to the story of the *Belgica*. It was a tale that Shackleton knew well, and he didn't hesitate to tell it to the crew.

In 1898 the *Belgica* became the first ship to winter below the Antarctic Circle. During her long, dark days stuck in the ice, a Belgian sailor died. The ship's officers gave him a burial at sea, sliding his body through a hole in the ice. The image haunted the men—their shipmate disappearing into the frigid waters. In the eerie half-light, they became convinced the dead man's body was following the ship, drifting beneath the ice. "We are under the spell of the black Antarctic night," wrote Frederick Cook, an American explorer on board, "and like the world which it darkens, we are cold, cheerless, and inactive."

As the dark days dragged on, the men sunk deeper into gloom. They heard the dead sailor's ghost in the creaks and groans of the *Belgica*'s timbers. After a while, the ship's cat seemed to lose its will to live. One day it curled up in a corner and died. With their lone predator gone, rats came out of the woodwork and ran wild. The sailors stuffed cloth in their ears, but the muffled sound of little claws on wood still tormented them through the night. Eventually, two men grew so agitated they had to be restrained.

The sailors of the *Belgica* were saved by the return of the sun—and by long hours of backbreaking labor. In January 1899, they hacked and sawed a 2,000-foot lead out of the ice. The *Belgica* sailed into open waters, and the crew returned to Europe, where the sun can be trusted to come up 365 days a year.

With the *Belgica* in mind, Shackleton fought the winter blues with work, a strict routine, and fun. Every day like clockwork the men gathered in the Ritz for meals: breakfast at 9 a.m., lunch at 1 p.m., tea at 4 p.m., and dinner at 6 p.m. Worsley once came in from a ski a few minutes late for lunch. He heard about it from the Boss.

At first, the men ate well—Shackleton made sure of it. There might be porridge, liver, and bacon for breakfast; a seal stew the sailors called "hoosh" for lunch; and seal steak for dinner with black currant tart for dessert.

Lees fretted over how fast the food was disappearing, but Shackleton insisted: A well-fed crew was a happy crew. Lees consoled himself by keeping a close eye on the supplies. He made sure he had a bunk near the storeroom door so he could pounce on thieves looking for a midnight snack.

At night, the Ritz became a clubhouse with a regular entertainment schedule. On Saturdays they drank and remembered their loved ones at home. On Sunday nights they listened to music on the phonograph while they went to bed. Sometimes the meteorologist Hussey led sing-alongs on his banjo. They held competitions to see who had the most annoying voice. "It is astounding the musical talent we do not possess!" Hurley observed.

A midwinter morning in the Ritz: To the left, the carpenter, McNish, works on a crib-
bage board and Blackborow hauls in a block of ice for drinking water. On the right,
Hussey, Huberht Hudson (standing), Wordie, and Clark occupy themselves reading
while the physicist, James, tinkers with water samples from the ocean. Lees sits at
the typewriter, probably working on his diary.

During the dark winter days, the scientists and the officers read books and debated important topics. Many a dispute ended with one party digging out a volume of the *Encyclopedia Britannica* to get a higher authority on his side.

But for all the knowledge the encyclopedia contained, it offered nothing on the most important subject of all: the war. Everyone aboard was desperate to know if their friends and family were safe from the fighting. All they could do was sit around a map of the world, make wild guesses, and plan imaginary battles by the light of an oil lamp.

———◆———

June was a cruel month at the bottom of the world.

The men kept close watch on their position in the ice. But it only reminded them how helpless they were. Their hope was to drift north toward the edge of the giant swirling pack of ice, where they might finally find open seas again. On June 8, they managed to make a little headway. "We have drifted 12 miles nearer Home & the Lord be thanked for that much as I am about sick of the whole thing," McNish grumbled to his diary that night.

As winter set in, the animals on the pack ice disappeared.

Worsley kept watch for a lone penguin or seal as best he could in the dim light. Night after night he recorded the results: "No animal life observed."

The entire landscape was dead. Except for the dogs.

Back in February, when it became clear they were going nowhere for the winter, Shackleton had divided the dogs into teams for training with the sleds. Wild, Hurley, the artist Marston, the doctors Macklin and James McIlroy, and the rugged second officer Tom Crean each got a team. The dogs were unruly and always entertaining. They became a spark of life in the darkness.

Crean had been a devoted dad to a litter of puppies since January. He was a big, burly Irishman who had been at sea since the age of 16 and survived two trips to the Antarctic already. But when the pups were born, he couldn't resist them. It wasn't unusual to find Crean with his pipe clenched between his teeth and his brawny arms wrapped around a couple of balls of fluff. The puppies got so attached to him that they wailed whenever he left and calmed down as soon as he came back.

Crean and the other dog "owners" treated their teams like spoiled children. They snuck extra food to their dogs and praised them to anyone who would listen. Each owner knew for a fact that his team was smarter and faster than the rest.

Crean and his pups: (clockwise from left) Roger, Toby, Nelson, and Nell.

On June 14, a debate broke out at lunch. Hurley, the proudest of the dog owners, insisted his team was far and away the fastest. His team leader, a giant sheepdog mix named Shakespeare, was a "magnificent animal," a "noble creature." With Shakespeare in command, Hurley boasted, no team could measure up to his.

The next day, he got a chance to prove it. In the dead darkness of winter, the entire crew gathered on the ice for the "Great Antarctic Derby." A few of the sailors dressed as bookies and took bets. Worsley wagered his week's ration of chocolate on Wild and his team leader, Soldier. The geologist Wordie put his ration on Hurley and the noble Shakespeare.

The teams started a half mile away and raced one at a time against the clock. A line of oil lamps marked the path to the finish line, near the ship. Shackleton started each team with the flash of a light. Worsley gave the play-by-play in his diary: "Somewhere in the crowd a pup yelps—a scientist swears . . . but presently the cry of 'Here they come!' is raised & something is seen moving swiftly ahead . . . Wild yells again & the pace becomes terrific. Soldier crouching low, head stretched forward & ears flapping in the breeze, dashes past the post in fine style, 2m 16 secs from the start."

The performance was enough to make Wild the winner. Hurley had to eat his words for now. He took second and insisted on a rematch.

The true winner, however, was Shackleton. For one day, he had brought his 27 men together, made them care about something, and given them a temporary victory over the coldest, darkest place on Earth.

———◆———

A month later, the Antarctic began to take its revenge. On Wednesday, July 14, the men woke to the sound of a gale screaming in the ship's rigging. The temperature plummeted to −33 degrees. Blinding curtains of snow raked the ship all day and into the night. Winds tore across the ice at 60 or 70 miles an hour. To feed the dogs, the men had to crawl to the dogloos. If they stood up, the wind knocked them down like they were made of straw.

The next day, the blizzard let up enough for the crew to survey the damage. Drifts of snow had climbed 14 feet to the ship's gunwales. The dogloos on the port side lay buried under 5 feet of powder. The men covered every inch of skin and waddled into the wind to dig their beloved dogs out.

At the height of the blizzard, Shackleton, Wild, and Captain Worsley gathered in the Boss's cabin. The wind sounded to Worsley like a train racing through the room at top speed. In the early hours of the morning, the ship had taken an unnerving jolt from below. Shackleton had told McNish it was probably a whale giving the hull a friendly nudge. But the Boss knew what it really meant. It was the ice, beginning to test the walls of the *Endurance*.

With the crew, Shackleton always tried to stay positive. But Wild and Worsley were his two most important officers; he could be honest with them. The Boss paced the room with his shoulders hunched and his hands behind his back. Worsley recognized the posture. He knew there was bad news to come.

"She's pretty near her end," Shackleton said.

"You mean that the ship will—go?" Worsley asked.

"I do," Shackleton responded.

Worsley refused to believe it. The ship had held up so far, and he couldn't imagine things getting worse than they had been for the last couple of months.

"You seriously mean to tell me the ship is doomed?" he said.

That was exactly what Shackleton meant.

"It may be a few months, and it may be only a question of weeks, or even days," the Boss said. "But what the ice gets, the ice keeps."

CHAPTER 6

EVICTED

The sun came back, and it brightened more than just the sky. In the middle of August five hours of real light shone on the crew every day. The ship drifted north at a good pace. By the end of the month they'd moved 300 miles closer to civilization.

As the weather warmed and the ship edged toward open water, the men started to think that the expedition wasn't dead after all. If the pack broke up soon, they could go back to Buenos Aires or South Georgia for provisions. Then they could make another run for Vahsel Bay.

At night in the Ritz, they guessed at the date they would finally break out of the ice. McIlroy put his money on November 3. Lees, who could be counted on to see the worst in a good situation, bet they'd be stuck until mid-February. Shackleton, always the optimist, claimed they'd be out by October 2.

The ice had given them a scare at the beginning of August. The floes shifted and squeezed together, rocking the ship and turning the dogloos into powder. Now at times they could hear the sea ice, restless in the distance. They struggled to describe the sounds—to relate the groaning and roaring to something they knew. It was like traffic in the streets of London. It was a giant train with squeaking axles, straining across the ice. Throw in steam whistles and roosters crowing. Under it all, Worsley heard the "moans and groans of souls in torment."

But near the end of September, life returned to the ice. Wordie saw an emperor penguin and lured it out of the water. The next day, Wild shot their first seal in five months. On September 29, two petrels rode the air currents over the ship. Since petrels feed in the sea, Lees observed, open water couldn't be far away. "My birthday," McNish recorded that day, "and I sincerely hope to spend my next one at Home."

Spring fever was working its way through the drafty passageways of the *Endurance*. They'd been on board more than a year and hadn't seen open water since January. Now, long cracks split the ice floes around the ship. Leads of dark water striped the vast canvas of white.

Shackleton decided it was time to move from the Ritz back on deck to their "summer cabins." McNish, who was

The men needed freshwater for drinking, cooking, and washing. To keep themselves supplied they sawed chunks off the surface of the sea ice, where snow
had fallen, compressed, and frozen. On board, the ice had to be melted over a
coal or blubber fire.

convinced they would be sailing again any day now, got to work putting bunks back in the old quarters. "The ship reverberates with hammers, sawing, cheers and song," Hurley wrote on October 12.

Two days later the ice split beneath the ship and for the first time in 8 months, they sailed through 100 yards of open water.

It would be the final voyage of the *Endurance*.

———•———

At 4 p.m. on October 18, the officers and scientists were drinking tea belowdecks when they felt the ice nudging the hull of the ship. It was enough to send the men ambling on deck to see what was happening.

As soon as they emerged, all hell broke loose. A wall of ice climbed the starboard side of the ship. The deck lurched underfoot and pitched to one side. In five seconds the *Endurance* tilted 30 degrees to port, and everything that wasn't nailed down started to slide. Kennels, sleds, crates, lumber, and men careened down the deck. James, the physicist, landed under two crates of clothing with a mass of frightened dogs howling on top.

Worsley stopped himself at the side of the ship and leaned out over the edge. He watched as the port side of the hull sank, inch by inch into the ice. Just when it seemed the ship would roll onto her side and give in, all movement stopped. The ship's captain brimmed with pride. "She seemed to say to the grinding hungry pack, 'You may smash me, but I'm damned if I'll go over another inch for you; I'll see you melting in Hell first.'"

The men spent the next two hours cleaning up as best they could. They nailed boards to the deck so they could walk without sliding into the mess jammed against the port gunwales. Then they liberated the dogs from the pile of kennels and secured the gear that hadn't already moved.

When everything on deck had been stabilized the crew gathered in the wardroom for a meal. Hurley managed to get a laugh out of the seating arrangement. Everyone sat on the floor with their feet jammed against freshly nailed boards. They balanced their food on their knees. Occasionally someone would forget their predicament, put a plate down on the floor, and watch it career into the port sidewall.

At 9 p.m., the ice shifted. The ship righted itself, and the men were once again walking on level ground.

The next day a killer whale almost as big as a bus surfaced in the tiny pool around the ship. All evening, the sleek predator swam from one end of the pool to the other. It poked its head above water, disappeared, and then rose again. "He was a cruel looking shark-like beast quite capable of swallowing one of us at a single gulp," Lees wrote.

And they could no longer count on the ship for protection.

———◆———

The final wave of pressure arrived at 6:45 p.m. on October 24. It moved through the pack slowly, squeezing the ship between giant slabs of ice. Macklin couldn't watch. "The whole sensation," the doctor wrote, "was of something colossal, of something in nature too big to grasp."

The crew soon realized that the sternpost—the giant pillar of wood that anchored the rudder to the rear of the ship—had been battered. Seawater was gushing into the stern.

McNish went back to start walling off the leak. Worsley and two others went below to get the main water pump working. A team climbed onto the floe to cut away the ice around the ship. But as soon as they cleared a section it froze again.

They got a day's rest from the pressure, but on October 26, the ice closed in again. Shackleton ordered everyone to get the essential gear onto the floe. Down went the three lifeboats, the sleds, the harnesses, and the tents. Worsley tore maps out of the ship's library books so they

Young emperor penguins pay a visit to the ship.

could leave the heavy volumes behind. Marston, Lees, and James hauled crates out of the hold with the sound of water rushing under them. Beams cracked like pistols overhead.

That night, the penguins popped up from the frozen sea and sang their strange, mournful dirge at the ship.

———◆———

At 4 p.m. the next day, a pressure ridge bore down on the starboard side of the ship. With one surge, the ice slipped under the *Endurance*, lifting her by the stern, and then by the bow. With the next surge, the floe climbed the side of the ship and broke off, sending blocks weighing as much as trucks tumbling backward. The surges followed, one after another. With each blow came a thunderous crash as the ship was tossed first to port, then to starboard.

Hurley set up his motion picture camera on the ice, expecting any minute to record the complete destruction of the *Endurance*.

Lees looked on with a sick feeling in his stomach. The ship was as powerful as any wooden vessel afloat. Now the ice was tearing her apart, plank by plank.

Finally, the deathblow came. The ship sat high out of the water, with the already damaged rudder exposed. A tumbling mass of ice swept across the stern and ripped the rudder and sternpost clean out of the ship. Giant timbers snapped with the sound of artillery guns firing into the air.

McNish emerged from below. The water was gaining on the pumps, he said. It wouldn't be long before the ship's boiler was swamped.

Shackleton, watching from the ice with Captain Worsley, gave the order to get the rest of the supplies down. The men lowered crates of food and bags of clothing while the ship heaved under their feet.

The Boss smoked cigarettes and mingled with the men. He reminded people not to forget one thing or another, as though they were packing for a weekend away.

"Mind you put your old diary in my bag," he said to Lees, "as it has been kept rather more regularly than mine, I believe."

Someone stretched a broad piece of canvas from the deck to the ice. One by one, the dogs were lifted into it and they slid, stumbled, and tumbled to safety. They were strangely quiet through the operation, as though they understood the importance of the moment.

By dinnertime, tents sprouted from the ice a safe distance from the ship. The temperature dropped to −15 degrees, and the men settled in to shiver in their sleeping bags. The nights in the Ritz, boring as they were, seemed like paradise now. There would be no more coal fire keeping them warm at night, no more sturdy hull between the men and the frozen sea. "We are homeless and adrift on the ice," Hurley wrote.

Shackleton stayed up to pace the ice. Before going to bed, Lees went up to him and tried to make conversation. With the work done for now and no orders to give, the Boss had sunk into a different mood than he'd been in a few hours earlier.

"I hope you haven't lost that cigarette case," Lees said, thinking of a beautiful gold case Shackleton carried.

Shackleton (right) and Worsley on deck, watching the relentless advance of the sea ice.

"Cigarette case be blowed," the Boss snapped. "I've just lost a bally ship haven't I?"

Shackleton was feeling the strain, and Lees understood why. Their best hope at this point was to drag the lifeboats toward open water. But the ice was a minefield of jagged pressure ridges and open leads. It would be tough going even without all the gear they had to haul. And even if they could navigate the sea ice, where would it get them? Besides their weather-beaten crew of 28 men, the only land creatures for 1,000 miles around were penguins and seals.

Then, of course, there was the food supply. Lees was in charge of rationing what they had, and he often felt like Shackleton would use it up in feast after feast, just to keep the men happy. Despite their efforts to salvage everything, tons of food was trapped in the ship under many feet of water. How long could they get by on what they had?

Later that night, in the cold comfort of a tent on the ice, Lees got out his diary and wrote, "For the first time in my life, we realized that we were face to face with one of the gravest disasters that can befall a polar expedition."

CHAPTER 7

"SHE'S GONE"

In the morning, after a steaming pot of hoosh had been ladled out and consumed, Shackleton gathered everyone on the floe. He'd been pacing the ice all night, but he was calm and matter-of-fact when he laid out the plan. "As always with him, what happened had happened," Macklin explained. "Without emotion, melodrama, or excitement, he said, 'Ship and stores have gone, so now we'll go home.'"

As usual, it wasn't as simple as he made it sound. Shackleton wanted to march 350 miles northwest to Paulet Island, near the tip of the Antarctic Peninsula. At Paulet Island, hopefully they would find a hut that had been stocked with supplies during the relief of the Nordenskjöld expedition. (Never mind that the supplies had been deposited there in 1903, more than 12 years ago.)

From Paulet Island, Shackleton could lead a small party

THE FATE OF THE ENDURANCE OCTOBER 1915

ARGENTINA

CHILE

DRAKE PASSAGE

Elephant Island

South Shetland Islands

Wilhelmina Bay

LARSEN ICE SHELF

Oct. 27, 1915: *Endurance* crushed

ANTARCTIC CIRCLE

ANTARCTIC PENINSULA

SOUTH PACIFIC OCEAN

—— Route of *Endurance*

---- Drift of *Endurance* in pack ice

▪▪▪▪ Planned trek across pack ice

0   200

MILES

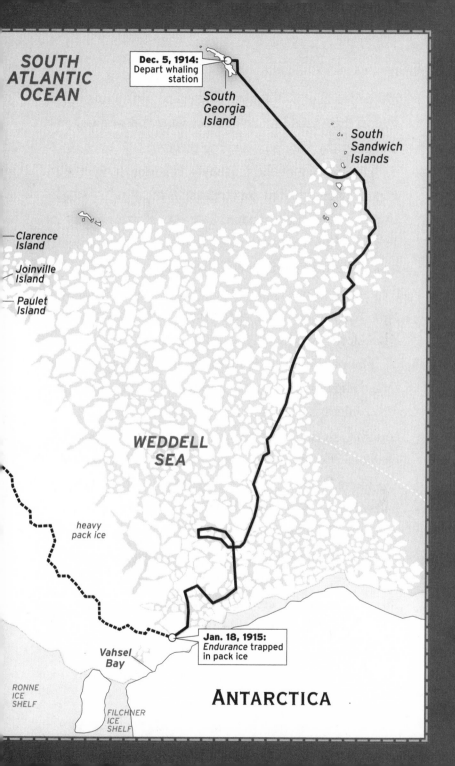

SOUTH
ATLANTIC
OCEAN

Dec. 5, 1914:
Depart whaling
station

South
Georgia
Island

South
Sandwich
Islands

Clarence
Island

Joinville
Island

Paulet
Island

WEDDELL
SEA

heavy
pack ice

Vahsel
Bay

Jan. 18, 1915:
Endurance trapped
in pack ice

RONNE
ICE
SHELF

FILCHNER
ICE
SHELF

ANTARCTICA

150 miles over 5,000-foot glaciers to Wilhelmina Bay. There, they would make contact with the whaling ships that used the bay as a stopping place.

The first leg of the journey was going to be grueling work. The crew had to drag thousands of pounds of supplies and two 1-ton lifeboats across an ever-shifting sea of ice. The supplies would travel by dogsled. But to move the boats, the men had to strap into harnesses and pull. If they made 6 miles a day, they might reach their goal by New Year's. Then they would have to get to Wilhelmina Bay before the whalers packed it in for the winter.

The plan was a long shot at best. But Shackleton had something besides rescue in mind. Even if they never made it to Paulet Island, he wanted the men to have a goal. They couldn't just sit down and wait like the crew of the *Belgica*. He needed them to feel like they controlled their fate.

There would be a strict weight limit for the trek—six pairs of socks, one spare pair of boots, one pair of fur mitts, one pound of tobacco or cocoa, and one pound of personal gear. In front of the men, the Boss took out the gold cigarette case that Lees had been so concerned about and dropped it on the ice. He added books, fifty gold coins, and a dozen other things to the pile.

Everyone else reluctantly followed suit. A heap of stuff accumulated on the ice, slowly disappearing under a blanket of snow. There were suitcases, clothes, cooking utensils, blankets, clocks, ropes, and tools. The only luxury allowed was Hussey's banjo.

Shackleton ordered one last sacrifice before they left. They couldn't afford to take McNish's cat or any of the puppies that hadn't been trained in harness, he said.

Big Tom Crean was devastated. The four pups that had been born in January were trained and part of a sled team. But he'd been caring for three more that weren't ready to pull a sled.

Macklin had another untrained pup named Sirius. A dreary shroud of snow fell on his head as he picked up a shotgun and took the pup aside. Sirius jumped up to lick his hand, and Macklin had to push him away. His hand was shaking so badly it took two shots to finish the dismal task.

———●———

They set off at 3 p.m. on October 30 in a long line across the ice. Shackleton, Hudson, Hurley, and Wordie led the way, choosing as level a path as they could find. The seven dog teams followed, carrying loads up to 700 pounds.

Bringing up the rear were 18 men, strapped into harnesses, straining to pull a 1-ton boat through wet snow and ice. McNish had built runners for the boats to help them glide across the pack. But instead, the boats sank in the slush. The men had to lean almost parallel to the ground to make progress. Every 15 minutes or so, they unstrapped and stood panting in the early summer air. Then they went back for the second boat.

For three hours they relayed their gear across the ice, a quarter mile at a time. The Boss didn't want the men spread out too far for fear the floe would split and leave the team separated for good.

At 6 p.m., the men saw smoke rising from a blubber fire ahead. They slogged through the final yards, sat down to eat, fell into their sleeping bags, and slept. "All are in high hopes," Hurley claimed, "and glad a start has been made from the depressing neighborhood of the wreck."

But there was still plenty to be depressed about. The exhausting labor of the first day left the ship's "neighborhood" just a mile behind. The men spent the night on new ice with killer whales spouting in the leads around them. The next day they dragged their burdens half a mile through a bed of fresh snow before giving up. The third day they tried again. They sank hip-deep in the slush until the Boss finally ended the torture.

The plan he laid out with such confidence a few days ago had failed.

They found a spot on an old floe that felt solid underfoot. The tents went up again, and they named their new

home Ocean Camp. After three days of backbreaking labor, they were 1½ miles closer to civilization.

That night, Lees sat in a tent with his diary. He was soaked to the bone and shivering, and yet he managed to sound almost optimistic. "So long as we have the bare minimum of food we shall be all right," he wrote.

As a statement of faith in their future, it wasn't exactly up to Shackleton's standards. But it would have to do.

Lees had been obsessed with the food supply for months. Now he had company. With the failure of Shackleton's epic trek, no one knew how long they would be on the ice. Everything depended on the whim of the pack. If the winds blew them northwest, they would make for Paulet Island again over land. If they drifted northeast, they would hit open water and launch the lifeboats.

But what if they stalled exactly where they were? Shackleton refused to admit it openly, but they could be spending another winter on the ice. By his own calculations, they only had enough food to last till March, the very beginning of the Antarctic winter.

Just when they had to think about rationing their food supply, the men became ravenously hungry. The human body, after all, wasn't built for the cold. Unlike cold-blooded fish or reptiles, humans need to keep an internal temperature of 98.6 degrees. The body starts cooling when the temperature outside drops below 78. The men now had a living environment that ranged from barely above freezing to −30 degrees. And they had no escape. There was no Ritz with a cozy stove to huddle around after hunting seals on the ice.

To keep their body temperatures from plummeting, they had to move constantly. They chased seals on skis or exercised the dogs or stood around and stamped their feet. Shivering alone can generate five times more heat than standing still.

But everything they did to keep themselves from freezing to death required calories—and that meant massive amounts of food. After a few days on the ice, the men became obsessed with meals. "All we seem to live for and think of now is food . . ." wrote Worsley.

The cook started throwing slices of seal blubber—pure fat—onto the stove or mixing it in the hoosh. The men devoured it and clamored for more.

With the men obsessing about food, all eyes turned to the *Endurance*. They had clung to their hope for her survival right up to the end. As a result, several tons of supplies still sat packed in water-tight crates in the storeroom. But retrieving them wasn't going to be easy. The crates lay submerged under 12 feet of water.

While they settled into Ocean Camp, half the crew took the dog teams back to the ship to see what they could salvage. The *Endurance* looked more like a junk heap than a vessel. Her main mast had cracked near the deck and fallen into a tangle of ropes. Twenty-foot spars had broken off entirely and lay caught in the rigging like twigs in a spider's web. The men had to take masts down and haul timbers away before it was safe to work.

For two days they dragged loads of wood, canvas, and cooking pots back to camp. Hurley stripped to the waist and dove into four feet of water to get his camera negatives. Someone salvaged part of the *Encyclopedia Britannica*. Six pounds of lentils, 7 pounds of oatmeal, and a can of soup made it off of the ship.

But after three days of labor, the bulk of the food still lay deep underwater. The men had to wade waist-deep just to stand on the deck over the storeroom.

At this point, the entire crew turned to McNish. The carpenter, blunt and ornery, infuriated Lees. Shackleton didn't trust him. No one quite knew whether he belonged with the officers or the sailors. But at times like this it became only too clear that they couldn't live without him.

A dog team rests before hauling supplies to camp from the broken ship.

On November 4, four days after the failure of their epic trek, McNish organized a team at the ship. He rigged a battering ram by tying one of the heavy, 3-inch-thick ice chisels to a rope and threading the rope through a pulley hung over the deck. One man hoisted the iron chisel high. Then he let it fall with a crash on the deck, just over the storeroom.

Again and again, they battered the decking until a crack appeared big enough to fit a saw. When they had sawed out a 3-foot-square hole, they moved the battering ram and made another hole. Then they replaced the chisel with a large hook, snagged the planks in between the holes, and ripped a huge chunk of the deck away.

It was 11 a.m. when food started bobbing to the surface. A cheer went up as loose walnuts and onions rushed through the hole. Then came the crates. The men worked with long boathooks, arms submerged to the shoulders in icy water, steering boxes toward the hole. It was brutal work, but one by one, crates of sunken treasure appeared. There were supplies of flour and sugar and tea. There were boxes of nut food—a tasty candy bar–like snack made of ground nuts, sugar, and sesame oil. There were crates of sledding rations, the dense mixture of beef, oatmeal, salt, sugar, and lard they had intended for the overland trek. When someone snagged an especially coveted box, the hungry, homeless men sent a cheer into the frigid air.

By the end of the day, 105 crates—3 tons of food—stood stacked on the ice at Ocean Camp. Thomas Orde-Lees was a happy man. "What this means to us in our present destitution," he wrote, "words fail to express."

———◆———

The salvage operation, it turned out, happened just in time.

McNish was convinced that all their disasters came on Sundays, and Sunday, November 21 seemed to prove his point. The men settled down in the late afternoon, trying to get comfortable enough on their sleeping bags to read. At 5 p.m. they heard the Boss's voice yell, "She's going!"

In a minute, everyone was on the ice, scrambling for a view. The sailors had built a 20-foot lookout tower out of wood scavenged from the ship, and that's where Shackleton stood. In the distance, he could see that the stern of the *Endurance* had been thrust high in the air. In a few minutes, it began to disappear. The entire ship—what was left of her—slipped bow first under the ice.

"She's gone, boys," Shackleton said quietly.

It didn't really qualify as a disaster. For Hurley, anyway, it was a relief. They had salvaged everything of value from the ship. Her creaking planks were a menace to anyone who tried to go aboard. The wreck was little more than a depressing reminder of their failure so far.

Even so, a silence fell over the camp. Bakewell, the American sailor who brought aboard his stowaway friend Blackborow, felt a lump in his throat as he watched the ship go. Lees felt like their last link to civilization had disappeared.

That night, Shackleton used a single sentence to record the event in his diary. Then he concluded, "I cannot write about it."

CHAPTER 8

A MISERABLE JOB

The morning after the wreck sunk, Lees added sausage to the breakfast menu. It wasn't like him to dole out luxuries so easily, but he thought a treat might add a little cheer to a dreary morning. If he was hoping it would also earn him praise from the Boss, he was wrong. Shackleton told him the sausages were too small and ordered him to give each man 2 instead of 1½. Lees gave in, but only after a lengthy battle at 7 in the morning. To get back at Shackleton, he took ham off the dinner menu.

It was a petty squabble—two grown men fighting over what amounted to 14 sausages. They had far bigger things to worry about. But both Lees and Shackleton knew how uncertain their future had become. To Shackleton, that meant doing whatever he could to keep the men from losing hope. To Lees it meant that 14 sausages might one day make the difference between starving to death and living to another sunrise.

———◆———

Mealtime became a primitive affair on the ice. The men had scavenged sails and spars from the *Endurance* and built a tent to serve as a galley. Inside was a stove that Hurley made out of an old ash chute from the ship. The cook, Charles Green, used strips of seal or penguin blubber for fuel. He fried seal steaks in blubber and cooked hoosh in an old oil drum. For plates the men used lids from biscuit tins or pieces of wood ripped from old crates. They ate

Lees, the storekeeper, and Charles Green, the cook, labor over a pot of hoosh on their makeshift stove.

hoosh in aluminum mugs. When they finished, grease and fragments of seal meat flavored their tea. Each man counted his spoon and his pocketknife as his most precious possessions.

At breakfast, lunch, and dinner, one man from each tent brought rations from the galley. He doled out portions while a tentmate closed his eyes and called out names randomly. Even then, the men couldn't help comparing their share to the others. An extra piece of blubber in a neighbor's hoosh was enough to make a hungry man burn with envy.

Most of the men devoured their food as soon it was handed to them. Lees, however, saved scraps obsessively. He stashed away hunks of cheese or pieces of bannock—a fried dough that became a delicacy as the flour started to run low. Lees drove everyone crazy by pulling random snacks out of his pocket when no one else had access to food.

The tents were a miserable substitute for the bunks in the Ritz. The men slept head to toe like sardines in a can. At night, their breath condensed on the canvas walls and froze into crystals that fell on their heads like snow. On days when the sun shone, the temperature in the tents could rise into the 60s, turning the snow under their sleeping bags to slush. Floorboards salvaged from the wreck kept them somewhat dry. But many of those boards had been torn from the dog kennels. It wasn't always clear what was to blame for the stench in the tents—the boards or multiple pairs of socks that hadn't been washed in two months.

After a couple of weeks on the ice, Lees was ejected from his tent because the men couldn't stand his snoring. Worsley called it his "nasal trombone." They had already suffered through months of loud rumblings in the Ritz. One night in May, when Hurley and Hussey were on watch, they had found Lees on his back snoring at top volume. They stuffed sardines and dry lentils in his gaping mouth to make him stop. Now, in the confines of a tent, the snoring became unbearable. Lees accepted his exile without too much resentment. The sailors had built a storeroom out of timbers from the wreck, and he made his own private bedroom there.

November turned to December. The midnight sun returned. The men did what they could to stay busy. McNish labored to make the lifeboats seaworthy. He built up the sides of the *Caird*, the largest of the three, using Marston's paints and seal's blood to caulk the boards. Hurley stayed spirited as always. He tinkered with a bilge pump for the *Caird* to keep the boat from getting swamped with water if they ever tried to launch it. He read novels and what was left of the encyclopedia. He exchanged stories with Shackleton. They even planned a new polar expedition for the future.

In the tents, the men held a running debate about their fate. Lees, true to form, figured they wouldn't reach the edge of the pack till June. Shackleton called him a pessimist—the worst insult possible in the Boss's view. They might find open water any day, Shackleton insisted. On December 8, they practiced loading the *Caird* and launching it in a small lead.

A week later they'd drifted to within 230 miles of Paulet Island. But they were farther east than Shackleton wanted to be. If they got a chance to launch the lifeboats, they would have to fight a strong west-to-east current in order to reach Paulet Island or the narrow strip of icy islands just north of it known as the South Shetlands.

If they couldn't reach Paulet, they weren't sure what they would do. There were two more tiny specks of land on the north edge of the Weddell Sea—Elephant Island and Clarence Island. Neither of them were inhabited. The men might find solid ground there and a few penguins or seals to feed them for a while. But the nearest human beings would still be 800 miles away at the whaling stations on South Georgia—800 miles of the most treacherous seas on the planet.

Ocean Camp, with the tower in the background where Shackleton stood to watch the remains of the *Endurance* disappear under the ice.

On December 21, Shackleton gathered everyone on the ice to announce yet another plan. As soon as they could pack the dogsleds, they would march again, directly west. This time, they would travel in the early morning and at night, when the surface had frozen into solid terrain. When he looked around, he thought he saw eager faces—men who were thrilled to have a goal after weeks of sitting around. But grumbling could be heard through the thin walls of the tents that night. "As far as I have seen the going will be awful," wrote the first officer Lionel Greenstreet, "and I sincerely hope he will give up the idea directly."

They held an early Christmas feast on December 22. For a single day it was all you can eat. There were sausages *and* ham for breakfast; baked beans and anchovies for lunch; canned rabbit, canned peaches, and an unlimited supply of jam for dinner. Lees knew they couldn't carry the food with them, but he couldn't help venting to his diary that night: "I hate to see so much good food being recklessly consumed."

At 4:30 a.m. the next day they were under way, stomachs groaning from the feast. But stomach pains were the least of their worries. The ice was treacherous, even in the colder hours. Cracks opened under the sleds; the dogs fell into open leads. The men sunk to their hips while hauling the lifeboats and had to be pulled out by their harnesses.

Once again, they ferried the boats in a relay, supervised by Worsley. This time, the ice was shifting so rapidly underfoot that they moved in 60-yard stretches. Every 20 yards they had to stop, lean on their knees, and catch their breath. By the time they returned for a boat, the slush had often frozen solid around its runners.

After a few hours each day, the men were exhausted and soaked to the bone with sweat and seawater. They scoured the horizon ahead for a piece of canvas stretched across a pole—the telltale sign that the cook had set up his galley and the end was in sight for the day.

One day, before he crawled into his sleeping bag, Worsley stripped to his long underwear and hung his pants and socks on a boat to dry. When he woke up they were frozen solid. There wasn't a thing he could do except beat the excess ice off of them and put them on.

They had reached their fourth day of torture when a sailor made his way to the front and found Shackleton. Captain Worsley had a problem in the rear and needed the Boss's help.

Shackleton trudged back and found the Skipper in a standoff with McNish. The carpenter was older than most of the men—in his early forties. He was exhausted, he was surly as always, and he was flat-out refusing to go any farther. What he was going to do instead was unclear. He wouldn't have survived a month on the ice by himself. But right now that didn't matter. He insisted he would not spend another minute as a beast of burden.

Worsley had already reminded McNish of his duties, but the carpenter insisted that he didn't have any. He had signed on as a sailor, he said. Now that the ship was gone, he had no obligation to follow anyone's rules but his own.

Shackleton immediately put that idea to rest. He told McNish firmly that he was committing mutiny by disobeying orders. In a polar expedition, the crew was bound to follow orders at sea or on land. McNish was being paid until the expedition ended, and until then he would obey the expedition's leader and its officers. If he chose not to he would be "legally punished." It was a threat that did not need to be explained. Under British law, mutineers could be shot to death by their commanders.

When Shackleton finished his lecture, he decided not to demand an answer right away. He let the carpenter go off and stew for a while. In the meantime he gathered the rest of the crew and told them exactly what he had told McNish. If pessimism could spread through an expedition like a contagious disease, Shackleton believed, rebellion could do the same. And if the crew refused to follow orders, the consequences could be fatal to them all.

A couple of tense hours passed, and no one stepped up to join McNish's revolt. Finally, the carpenter had no choice but to get back in his harness and pull.

The next day, he got what he wanted anyway. Shackleton and Hurley scouted the ice ahead. They found it soft, unstable, and scarred with pressure ridges. Shackleton wanted desperately to keep the men moving, but the terrain was too risky. He returned to the tents and announced they would make camp.

Once again, they were back to Plan B: wait and watch.

Shackleton called their new home "Patience Camp." But at this point, patience was wearing thin.

For his part, Shackleton had already put the failed march behind him. He acted as though the new plan—do nothing until the ice freed them—was better than the old. And until now, his unshakeable confidence had held the crew together.

But after the third change in plans, McNish wasn't the only one losing faith in Shackleton. "The Boss at any rate has changed his mind yet once again," the geologist Wordie wrote their first night in Patience Camp. "He now intends waiting for leads, and just as firmly believes he will get them, as he did a week ago that the ice would be fit for sledging the boats at the rate of ten miles a day."

To the men it now seemed likely they would have to winter on the ice, and they began to watch the hunting trips with great anticipation. To make it through a winter, they needed seal and penguin meat put away by the ton. But Shackleton didn't seem to feel the urgency. In early January 1916, Lees came back to camp after shooting three seals. The Boss wouldn't dispatch a sled to pick up the carcasses. They had a month's supply of meat now, he said. The ice was soft, and he didn't want to risk the trip.

Lionel Greenstreet fumed. Nothing so far, he reflected, had turned out the way Shackleton predicted. "His sublime optimism all the way through," the first officer wrote, "is to my mind absolute foolishness."

By January 13, word got around that Shackleton had made a decision to kill at least some of the dogs. Every day for four days, hunting parties had scoured the ice without spotting a seal. Their meat supply was dwindling, and it took one seal a day just to feed the dogs. Everyone knew it was only a matter of time, since they couldn't take the dogs on the lifeboats. But when they heard about the Boss's decision, it still came as a shock.

The next day, Wild, Marston, McIlroy, and Crean harnessed their teams and led them about a quarter mile away from camp. Macklin and McIlroy guided the dogs one by one behind a hill of snow, where Wild waited with a revolver. The dogs went willingly, their tails wagging, no idea what lay in store.

Wild had never in his life had a job as miserable as this one.

Back at camp, the men could hear the shots ring out across the ice, a grim reminder of just how desperate their lives had become.

CHAPTER 9

LASH UP AND STOW!

For four days, the wind blew in a gale from the southeast. By January 21 they had drifted 74 miles north, and Shackleton was feeling good again. "Lees and Worsley are the only pessimistic ones in the camp," he crowed, "but this strong wind even made Lees suggest larger steaks."

Then, as if nature had chosen sides in the running battle between the Boss and his storekeeper, the wind died.

Worse, the seals vanished. Hurley thought they had migrated south for the summer; McNish thought they had gone north. Either way, a critical source of food was gone.

For now, the men still had meat, but their supply of blubber for the stove was running painfully low. They had to shut down one of the galley fires, and that meant no hot milk at lunch. Drinking water had to be rationed since they couldn't afford the fuel to melt enough ice. The men started packing snow into cans and tucking them into their sleeping bags at night so they would have water by morning.

The sad crew of 28 men, stranded on the ice, were competitors in a race. But unlike any race they had ever witnessed, they had no influence on the outcome. On one side stood their food supply, on the other the ice. If the ice vanished before their food, they had a chance at victory.

Everything depended on the wind, and they became obsessed with each gust. They pestered Hussey, the meteorologist, for predictions, but he had nothing to tell them. Without help from science, they fell back on superstition. Mention the wind and you had to touch wood. The 7th of every month would bring good luck and gusts from the south, but beware the 13th.

On February 19, an army of little Adélie penguins appeared on the floe. The men turned out like medieval warriors with oars, pickaxes, and whatever else they could find for weapons. They surrounded the birds and slaughtered more than 300 of them. Most of the men could not have imagined themselves killing like this just a year ago. Now, hunger had hardened them. "The result was very satisfactory," Hurley wrote.

But the Adélie slaughter hardly meant a life of luxury for the hunters. Burning 20 penguin skins a day, they had fuel for 15 days. And the meat—two or three pounds per

Hurley skins a penguin with Shackleton at the Boss's tent while a block of ice melts in a stove between them.

bird—wouldn't feed 28 men for long. McNish sat with his diary that night and grumbled about their meager provisions. They celebrated the butchery with "stewed penguin heart, liver, eyes, tongues, toes and God knows what else," he wrote. "I don't think any of us will have nightmares from over-eating."

———◆———

March dawned cold, damp, and calm. Winter was bearing down again, and the weather ruled the daily routine. The hardship was relentless. When they relieved themselves in the snow, they wiped themselves with ice. Their eyes teared constantly in the wind. The tears froze into icicles at the tip of the nose, and when they swiped the ice away, pieces of skin came off with it. To wash with water meant risking frostbite. It had been four months since anyone had taken a bath, and no one had a change of clothes left.

The only relief from the cold was to crawl inside a sleeping bag and stay there—and that's what most of the men did, from six at night to eight in the morning. The boredom grew nearly intolerable. The only topic of conversation that drew any interest at all was the wind. Every other subject had been covered a hundred times over. "The monotony of life here is getting on our nerves," Greenstreet wrote. "Nothing to do, nowhere to walk, no change in

Drying laundry during another dismal day at Patience Camp.

surrounding, food or anything. God send us open water soon or we shall go balmy."

Stuffed into tents together 14 hours a day, the men did what they could to keep from strangling one another. The doctor Macklin lay down one night with his tentmates next to him and blasted each one of them in his diary. He was sick of Clark, who sniffed all the time. Lees, who was back in the tent now, snored "abominably." When he wasn't snoring, he did nothing but "argue and chatter" with Worsley about trivial things. "At times like this," Macklin complained, "with Clark sniff-sniffing into my ear, my only relief is to take up my diary and write."

On March 9, an extended blizzard finally let up, and the men emerged from the tents to enjoy their first time outside in three days. Captain Worsley went off on skis to look for a seal that had been left on the ice two weeks earlier. On his way back, he paused on a fragment of young ice. Beneath his feet he felt a swaying movement he hadn't felt in a year. As a sea captain, he knew the feeling well: It was the slow, rhythmic swelling of the sea. And if the swells were once again making their way through the ice, open water couldn't be far away.

Worsley hurried back to share his discovery. Everyone turned out on the ice and stared for hours into the slushy pools around the camp. They measured the height of the swells and the time between them. With a few calculations from the physicist James, they figured they were 20 to 30 miles from open water.

It was a welcome sight, this distant echo of the open ocean. But it also raised another fear. If the swells increased, they would bend and warp the floes. Eventually, the ice would give in and crumble under their feet. If that happened before open leads formed in the pack, they would be in deep trouble. The pack would be too fragmented to camp on and too tight to navigate. They would have no choice but to launch the lifeboats into a minefield of jagged ice.

On March 17, they consumed the last of the flour. The cocoa was gone. In a few days, the tea would be gone too. They had almost nothing to eat but meat and fat, and without carbohydrates in their diet, the men were getting weak. "Hunger is now our lot," Lees wrote. "Not starvation, but real hunger all day long."

The men started to covet food they wouldn't have touched a few months before. They drank pure oil rendered from blubber. They no longer had water to wash dishes, so the hoosh arrived with extra texture—penguin feathers or reindeer hair from the sleeping bags. No one seemed to care.

Worsley and Greenstreet started telling Marston, the plumpest of the crew, that he'd be perfect if they had to resort to cannibalism. "We implore him not to get thin and even go so far as to select chops, etc., off him and quarrel about who shall have the tenderest part," Worsley wrote.

Marston did not appreciate the humor. He did his best to avoid his tormentors when he saw them coming his way.

"Land in sight! Land in sight!" The cry rang out across the camp the morning of March 23. Shackleton had been peering west through the fog when he caught a glimpse of a mountain in the distance. There had been plenty of false alarms in recent weeks, so he called Hurley over, and the photographer agreed. They decided the mountain belonged to Joinville Island, at the tip of the Antarctic Peninsula. It was the first land they had seen in 14 months, and it couldn't have been more than 40 miles away.

Hurley could barely contain his excitement: "General rejoicing! If the ice opens we can land in a day."

But in fact, there was nothing to rejoice about. Joinville Island was uninhabited. And with no open water in sight, it was also unreachable. So was Paulet Island, which lay south of Joinville. Still stuck in the pack, the men were drifting helplessly past the northernmost edge of Antarctica. Another 100 miles north lay the stormy Drake Passage, the vicious stretch of open ocean just below the southern tip of South America. And all that remained between the Drake Passage and the crew were those two tiny, uninhabited specks in the sea: Clarence Island and Elephant Island.

The next day, Lees tilted his head to the sky and gazed at the birds with envy: "A flock of Dominican gulls passed over. Oh! had we but their wings."

The moment of decision came two weeks later. The swells Worsley noticed had grown into a menace. All around them, their once-stable floe had been wrenched into slabs of ice not more than 100 yards square. "[W]e are in the hands of a Higher Power," wrote Macklin, "and puny mortals that we are, can do nothing to help ourselves against these colossal forces of nature."

On April 9, they woke to find a new crack headed straight for the camp. The cry went up: "Lash and stow!" Shackleton ordered the tents struck and the supplies ready to load.

But even with the ground vanishing under their feet, no one wanted to launch. All around them treacherous chunks of ice churned in the current. Cracks opened and closed in an instant. Slabs of ice slapped together with enough force to crush their tiny lifeboats.

At 11 a.m., the pack left them no choice. A crack split the floe right where the tents had been, leaving the crew barely room to stand. They slid the boats awkwardly into the swells. Stumbling to keep their footing, the men hoisted crate after crate into the three boats. Lees knew their rations to the ounce: 24 cases of sledding rations, 13 cases of nut food, 11 cases of biscuits, two 72-pound bags of seal meat, and so on.

When the boats were full, they shoved off into the sea. It was the moment they had been dreaming of for months. But now that it had finally arrived, they felt lost. As hard as life had been on the floe, Shackleton thought, it had given them a sense of security. Now their home had shattered under their feet. They could see the peaks of Clarence Island and Elephant Island 60 miles to the north. But no one knew if they would ever get there.

CHAPTER 10

AN INFINITY OF ICE

All afternoon, the three wooden boats bobbed and weaved through the churning ice. Shackleton commanded the *Caird*, with Wild at the tiller. Worsley piloted the *Dudley Docker*. Hudson and Crean took charge of the *Stancomb Wills*.

Shackleton had decided they would head northwest for the South Shetland Islands. At the far western end of the island chain lay a C-shaped spit of land called "Deception Island." Supposedly, supplies and shelter had been left there for shipwrecked seamen. Whalers also used the island's bay as a summer way station. If the men were lucky, a stray ship or two might still be sheltering in the harbor.

Getting there, however, was going to be treacherous. The island was at least 150 miles to the west. In their path lay a minefield of sea ice. If the crew managed to clear the ice, open water might prove even more dangerous. High winds tormented the strait that separated the Antarctic Peninsula from the South Shetlands. Huge swells could easily swamp the 20-foot boats.

For now, they rowed their way through a confusing mix of slush, slabs of pack ice, and jagged hunks of broken bergs called "growlers." In the waning light they found a solid floe to camp on, about half the size of a football field.

Around 11 p.m., Shackleton was pacing the ice when he felt the floe lift on a swell and crack under the camp. The biggest tent crumpled as the ice beneath it gave way.

Shackleton rushed toward the tangle of canvas and yelled, "Are you alright?"

"There are two in the water!" came the reply.

The crack had opened 4 feet wide, and in the water between the two icy walls, Shackleton saw a white object, bobbing with the swells. He leaned down and grabbed a handful of reindeer skin. With the crack threatening to slam shut again, he heaved a sleeping bag and a struggling man to safety. The man was the young stoker Ernest Holness, who came out sputtering and furious that he'd lost his supply of tobacco to the sea. Seaman Walter How, the other man who had fallen in, had managed to pull himself back to solid ground.

The men spent much of the night huddled around a blubber fire, listening to killer whales blow in the leads.

They took turns walking Holness around to keep him warm. The ice on his clothes crinkled as he moved.

In the morning, giant hunks of ice surrounded their little island, slamming together on the swells. They kept a close watch and saw an opening at 8 a.m. The order went out

to launch, and once again the men leaned into the oars, staving off lumps of ice as they made their way through crowded channels of water.

After two hours, they emerged into long, rolling swells—not just a lead, but an unbroken expanse of water. For the first time since they left South Georgia 16 months

ago, it felt like they had found the open ocean. At first, Lees felt a grand sense of freedom to have left the pack behind.

Then he felt the morning's hoosh rise in his stomach.

The swells tossed the boats like toys, turning several of the men pale with seasickness. Still, they raised the sails for the first time in a stiff wind and made good time. In the *Docker* Worsley handed out a lunch of biscuits and uncooked dog pemmican—a dense mix of dried beef, ground beef, and fat. Lees could barely look at the raw meat.

With a wet, cold blizzard beginning to blow, Shackleton ordered the boats back into the edge of the pack in the late afternoon. They found a low berg, about 20 yards across, and camped for the night.

At dawn, Shackleton, Wild, and Worsley took turns climbing to the crest of their iceberg to look for open water. Giant swells swept through the pack, lifting their little camp 12 feet in the air and then dropping them deep into a trough with a sea of ice rising on either side. Hurley took a turn and saw an "infinity of ice-covered ocean-berg fragments, shattered floes and brash ice, heaving . . . and grinding, crunching, groaning into an indescribable chaos."

A couple of the men, sick from the constant motion,

vomited onto the ice. Others forgot the danger they were in, entranced by the spectacle around them.

Shackleton, however, did not forget. He watched while their floe disintegrated, hoping desperately to find an opening for the boats. He was convinced that he had finally led the men to their end.

Around noon, he decided they had to take a chance. The ice surrounding the floe loosened enough to get the boats into the water. They loaded up as fast as possible and launched. Lees looked back to see their floe collide with another, obliterating the channel they had just escaped with a "splitting, pulverising crash." They rowed furiously for a few minutes and cleared the treacherous belt of ice that had nearly ended their journey.

But once again, the hardship was just beginning.

———◆———

When darkness fell that night they found a floe, anchored the boats, and put the cook ashore to heat some milk. But while they started to unload the tents, the swells rose and the boats bobbed like corks. Shackleton gave the order to cast off before the churning sea dashed the boats against the floe. They would spend the night jammed into their boats, drifting aimlessly in the frozen pack.

For four months they had been stuck on the ice with no escape. Now they had been exiled from it for good. The cramped tents that had been their prisons just three days ago seemed like palaces next to the boats.

They spent the night huddled on the benches or in the icy bilge below. Spray and sleet soaked their clothing, froze instantly, and coated them in ice. They couldn't row to keep warm because the darkness hid the obstacles lurking in the water. Instead they jockeyed for position or held one another for body heat. One or two men staved off marauding chunks of ice with the oars. Others simply sat and groaned, trying to keep from losing their dinner into the sea.

When dawn finally broke, the men willed their frozen bodies to life. They leaned into the oars, drained from lack of sleep. The sky was clear, and at noon Worsley got out his instruments. With frost-numbed fingers, he measured their position.

For three days they had barely slept. They had lived on raw meat and cold biscuits. They had narrowly escaped being cast into 30-degree water and crushed by 10-ton slabs of ice. For all their efforts they had somehow drifted south and east of Patience Camp. They now found themselves farther from land than when they started.

The next day, Shackleton took a good look at the three crews and didn't like what he saw. The men looked terrible, lips cracked and bleeding, faces crusted in salt. Fingers had turned white from frostbite. Several of the crew had diarrhea from eating raw meat.

Deception Island was now out of the question. They had to make land fast, no matter the risk. Elephant Island and Clarence Island lay 80 miles away across treacherous seas. If they didn't get there fast, men would begin to die.

The Boss distributed crates of food to the *Docker* and the *Wills* and gave everyone freedom to eat their fill. Then he led the way recklessly through the ice. The men tried to fight off growlers with the oars. The *Caird* was gored by a piece of ice above the waterline but kept going.

By the time darkness fell they had hit open water, and the men spent a harrowing night at sea. Sheets of water sprayed the boats relentlessly. The temperature plummeted. The men in the *Wills* had to bail constantly to keep the water from freezing around the supplies in the stern. Even so, a thick crust of ice weighed down the boat, threatening to sink her in the dark. Every hour, someone had to chip away at the ice with an ax.

Even in the *Caird*, men were stretched to the breaking

point. They had no ice left to melt for drinking water, and thirst tormented them. Their tongues swelled in their mouths from dehydration, making it hard to eat. To Hurley, it seemed as though the torture would go on forever. "Never was dawn more anxiously awaited, never did night seem so long," he wrote.

Finally, the sun climbed above the horizon and glistened off the water, and as the morning brightened, a distinct grayish-white shape, and then another, rose from the water in the north. To the men it was the sight of hope itself— Clarence Island and Elephant Island looming in the distance, not more than 30 miles away.

———◆———

It took yet another day and night, but on the morning of April 15, they rowed beneath the cliffs of Elephant Island. The shore was nothing but sheer rock walls and ice, pounded by the sea. To Hurley the coastline looked "wild and savage beyond description."

Finally, they found a beach guarded by a treacherous-looking row of rocks. Shackleton decided they had to risk it. They had been rowing in half-hour shifts to stay warm. By the time each shift gave up the oars their hands were frozen to the handles. They had started chewing hunks of frozen seal meat to let the blood moisten their mouths.

Some of the men in the *Wills* looked like they wouldn't survive another half a day without water and a hot meal. Blackborow was losing his feet to frostbite, and the saltwater had worn painful boils into everyone's skin. Hudson had collapsed and was no longer making sense. Frank Wild decided that half the crew had gone insane from cold, hunger, thirst, and pure exhaustion.

The boats maneuvered across a narrow channel between the rocks until the hulls scraped solid land. Giddy with relief, Shackleton insisted Blackborow take the honor of stepping ashore first. The Boss had come to like the young stowaway and knew he'd had a hard time of it in the *Wills*. Apparently, he didn't know how badly frostbitten Blackborow's feet were. When Blackborow made no move to climb out, Shackleton nudged him over the side. Blackborow's feet failed to support him, and he promptly sat down in the frigid surf. He had to be carried onto the beach, where he sat while the men unloaded the boats.

Two hours later, smoke rose from a blubber stove in the middle of the rocky beach. On top of it, a pot of powdered milk simmered. Steaks from two freshly killed seals awaited room over the flames. Around the stove, the

Solid ground: hauling the *Caird* ashore on Elephant Island.

men kneeled on solid ground for the first time in more than 16 months. When they smiled, beads of blood rose through the cracks in their lips. They buried their faces in the rocks or gathered pebbles in their hands and let them trickle through their fingers. To Shackleton they looked like "misers gloating over hoarded gold."

CHAPTER 11

OUR ONLY HOPE

The men spent their first day on dry land moving crates, setting up tents, and eating. A herd of Weddell seals had welcomed them to the beach. In exchange for their hospitality, the cook went on a killing spree with an ax. When he was done, he served the weakest of the men first with hot milk. He spent the next hours frying seal steaks and blubber. The men ate them as fast as they came off the fire.

That night, they had trouble getting comfortable. The smooth bed of snow they'd slept on for six months had been replaced by a rocky beach. But a few rocks poking at their ribs seemed a small price to pay for the knowledge that the ground below could not crack and send them plunging into the sea.

Hurley, for one, was ecstatic: "How delicious to wake in one's sleep and listen to the chanting of the penguins

The first hot drink after a week at sea. From left: Lees, Wordie, Clark, the engineer Rickinson, Greenstreet, How, Shackleton, Blackborow's friend Bakewell, the engineer Kerr, and Wild.

mingling with the music of the sea. To fall asleep and awaken again and feel this is real. We have reached the land!!"

———◆———

But when the initial elation wore off it wasn't exactly clear what they had gained. Hurley and the rest of the men could count themselves pioneers of a barren wasteland. Elephant Island supports no year-round life besides the moss and lichens that cling to its rocks. Seals and penguins visit the island but desert it in the winter.

It didn't take the men long to realize they couldn't stay where they had landed. They could see watermarks on the cliffs at the back of the beach. When high tide came in they'd be swamped.

No one wanted to get back in the boats, but on April 16, the day after they landed, Shackleton sent Wild out in the *Wills* with four men to scout the coast. They found another haven, and the next day, the crew packed up the boats and moved. After a miserable six-hour sea journey they made camp yet again. They called their new home "Cape Wild."

They settled in as best they could. At least eight men were completely useless. The engineer, Louis Rickinson, had collapsed from a mild heart attack. Blackborow still couldn't walk. Hudson's hands hadn't recovered, nor had his brain. He lay in his sleeping bag, refusing to move.

As Greenstreet's hands came back from frostbite they blistered badly. On the boat journey to the new beach, the liquid in the blisters froze solid. When he came ashore he saw steam rising from freshly butchered seals. He stumbled over to a carcass and plunged his hands inside to warm them up.

Their new home was no more comfortable than the old one. Hurley said it was "like the courtyard of a prison only 250 yards by 50 yards wide." Cliffs 1,200 feet high and the icy slope of a glacier formed the walls of the prison. Penguin poop, known as guano to the seamen, carpeted the ground. Winds swept down from the cliffs powerfully enough to lift pebbles in the air. "A more inhospitable place could scarcely be imagined," Macklin concluded.

A five-day blizzard greeted them at Cape Wild, and it seemed as though some of the men had finally had enough. According to Wordie they had to be "dragged from their bags and set to work." Driving snow rushed down the throat with every breath. The first night in the new camp the wind shredded the largest of the tents, and the men had to pull the remains around them and huddle till dawn. McNish curled up with his diary the night of April 20 and made a prediction: "I don't think there will be many survivors if they have to put in a winter here."

In front of the men, Shackleton was as confident as ever. He knew that many of them were ready to give up, and it was his job to make sure they stayed motivated. "The boss is wonderful," Wordie wrote, "cheering everyone and far more active than any other person in camp."

In private, Shackleton struggled with the fear McNish had confessed to his diary. As the blizzard persisted, he took the doctor Macklin aside and asked him how long he thought the men would last on the island. At this point they had full rations for five weeks, maybe three months if they cut their meals to near starvation level. Seals and penguins would add to their supply, but no one knew when the animals would disappear for the winter. If the conditions didn't change, Macklin said, they'd start losing men in a month.

———◆———

The fifth day on Elephant Island, Shackleton confirmed the next plan, which was no surprise to the men. They had been talking about it since before they left Patience Camp. As soon as the weather cleared, the Boss would launch the *Caird* with a crew of five.

Cape Horn at the tip of South America and the Falkland Islands in the South Atlantic were the nearest targets. But they both lay north and west of Elephant Island while the current and the wind ran hard to the east. Shackleton didn't think they stood a chance of fighting their way north. Instead they would make the longer voyage east to South Georgia, find their way to one of the whaling stations, and return with a ship to carry the rest of the men back to civilization.

It could all be done, he claimed, in a month. They'd be back before the end of May.

Many of the men wondered if it could be done at all. They had traveled no more than 80 miles to get to Elephant Island and it nearly killed them. South Georgia lay 800 miles away across seas that had swamped far bigger boats than the *Caird*. "I would rather die than undertake such a journey," Lees confided to his diary.

Lees, and perhaps a few others, thought Shackleton was making a mistake. The whaling station at Deception Island lay 200 miles to the southwest across calmer seas. Lees thought that should be their target. But the Boss was convinced the pack was too dense to make the journey now. And the whalers had no doubt abandoned the harbor for the winter. The men would have to wait till September at the earliest to make the trip. Shackleton was convinced they didn't have that long.

———◆———

McNish went to work in the howling gale building a deck for the *Caird*. Right now she was open to the sky and the sea, and the men would never survive the journey exposed to the surf. With help from Marston and the old seaman McLeod, the carpenter scavenged wood and nails from the *Docker* and plywood from old crates. They used runners saved from one of the sleds to build a framework across the gunwales. They nailed boards on top for decking. Then they stretched canvas from the shredded tents across the entire thing, hoping it would keep most of the raging ocean out.

McNish had a personal stake in his work on the *Caird* because he would be aboard for the voyage to South

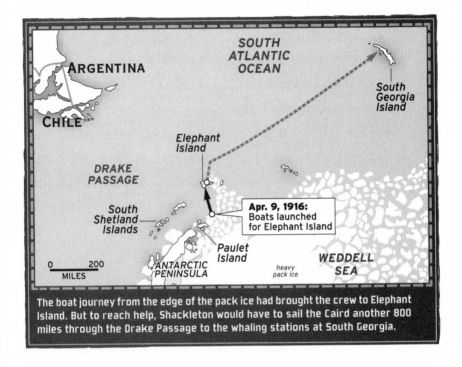

The boat journey from the edge of the pack ice had brought the crew to Elephant Island. But to reach help, Shackleton would have to sail the Caird another 800 miles through the Drake Passage to the whaling stations at South Georgia.

Georgia. For all his faults, the carpenter had proved himself essential to the crew several times over. If the *Caird* needed work in the middle of the Drake Passage, Shackleton wanted McNish aboard to do it.

For the rest of the crew, Shackleton chose Worsley for his navigation skills, the indestructible second officer Crean for his experience and his loyalty, and two hardy sailors named Timothy McCarthy and John Vincent.

All work came to a halt on April 22 when a blizzard

turned Cape Wild into a war zone. No one left his sleeping bag unless he absolutely had to. The men on mess duty could barely walk upright long enough to get food from the galley and hustle it back to the tents. Ice and gravel, tossed by the wind, slashed the skin on their faces. A 10-gallon aluminum pot went airborne and landed far out to sea. Socks, mittens, sheets, wood, and boots followed the same route. Lees lost a shirt even after weighing it down with two stones the size of a man's head.

———◆———

Two days later, the gale had finally died. Just after noon, 22 men stood on the shore of Cape Wild, watching the *Caird*'s sail lift on a swell and then vanish into a trough. The 22-foot boat carried four weeks' worth of food, two casks of water, a ton of rocks as ballast, and six men—including their leader, their navigator, and their carpenter.

According to Hurley they were "six proven veterans seasoned by the salt and experience of the sea." He had confidence they would make it to South Georgia in 14 days and return as planned. Then again, Hurley rarely expressed anything without confidence.

Wordie, who was more of a realist, watched the sea until the sail disappeared for the last time. He and the

Launching the *Caird* for South Georgia.

rest of the men turned back to their wind-swept prison with its walls of granite and ice. That night he went to bed thinking of the *Caird*. He tucked himself into his sleeping bag on a reeking bed of penguin guano, and wrote, "She is our only hope."

CHAPTER 12
ACROSS THE SEA

Their first night out in the *Caird*, Shackleton and Worsley sat up piloting the boat through the darkness. Worsley took the tiller and Shackleton huddled for warmth with his arm around the Skipper's shoulder. They had rowed their way through the first hazard of the voyage—the loose pack that surrounded Elephant Island. Now they were under sail, taking advantage of winds out of the south. They would sail as far north as they could to make sure they cleared the ice. Then they would ride the westerly winds toward South Georgia.

Shackleton was in a reflective mood. Alone with Worsley, he didn't have to bolster anyone's morale. In the dark he dropped the cloak of confidence he showed to the world and allowed the sound of pessimism to creep into his voice. He was sick with regret that he had to split up the party and leave 22 men behind. It was the only reasonable choice—he knew that. They couldn't simply camp on a barren island and wait until they starved to death. And if the voyage had to be made, as the leader of the expedition, he couldn't leave it to anyone else.

But it was a terrible choice to have to make, and now the fate of the men depended on the whims of the weather and the sea. Already, the stiff west-to-east current of the Drake Passage was making itself felt. They had sailed into the one place on Earth where the ocean circles the entire planet, unbroken by land. Winds lash the water at speeds up to 200 miles per hour. With no obstacle for 12,000 miles, waves known as "Cape Horn Rollers" can reach heights of 80 or 90 feet. The famous biologist Charles Darwin witnessed them when he sailed past Cape Horn, at the tip of South America, in 1834. "One sight . . . ," he wrote, "is enough to make a landsman dream for a week about death, peril and shipwreck."

The swells didn't approach 80 feet the night of April 24, 1916. But they were perilous enough. When they caught the *Caird* broadside they swamped her deck and sent saltwater streaming through McNish's handiwork. Less than 24 hours out, it was already clear they would spend the entire voyage soaked to the bone.

Shackleton rolled cigarettes, and they fought the wind and the spray to get them lit. He asked Worsley if he thought they'd made the right choice. If they headed for Cape Horn, they could cut the distance almost in half. Worsley assured him the wind would blow them too far east. South Georgia was the only reasonable target.

As the boat rode on into the dark, Shackleton asked again. Worsley gave him the same answer. It was an unfamiliar scene, someone offering reassurance to the Boss. But Shackleton obviously needed it. He felt responsible for the entire ordeal, starting with his decision 16 months earlier to pass up a landing at Glacier Bay and start the overland trek from there. His men now sat on Elephant Island with nothing to do but wait. He was in fact their only hope. If they didn't survive, he told Worsley later, he would feel like a murderer for the rest of his life.

———◆———

As the *Caird* disappeared into the waves on April 24, Shackleton's trusted friend and second-in-command Frank Wild was left guarding the survival of 22 men. And when the party turned to trudge back to camp, Wild noticed a couple of them crying. Someone said, "that's the last of them," and Wild felt like picking up a rock and knocking the pessimist down. Instead he spent a minute or two cursing him out.

Frank Wild was Shackleton's man, and he had taken up where the Boss left off, doing what he could to keep the men from sinking into despair. And like Shackleton, his most effective tactic was to put them to work.

On the 28th, the men gave up on their ragged tents and made a shelter out of the *Wills* and the *Docker*. It was grueling work for a crew that had been starved of carbohydrates for months on end. They hauled stones from 150 yards away and stacked them into walls four feet high. Lees said it took three men to haul a load normally fit for one. With the end walls in place, the boats were turned upside down to make the roof. Marston hung tent canvas from the gunwales of the boats for the sidewalls.

The *Wills* and the *Docker*, converted into a home for 22 men.

When it was done, the men jockeyed for positions inside. Ten of them immediately claimed the benches of the overturned boats for beds. The rest slept underneath on a thin carpet of canvas stretched over the pebbles and the penguin guano.

The finished structure was something to be proud of—until they woke the next morning buried in snow. Yet another blizzard had swept the beach during the night, finding every little imperfection in the hut. Boots were frozen so stiff they had to be put on in stages. The men brushed off the snow and sat on their sleeping bags, quietly cursing their miserable prison of rock and ice. "All attempts seemed so hopeless," Macklin wrote, "and Fate seemed absolutely determined to thwart us."

On April 26, two days into the *Caird*'s voyage, a westerly gale ripped into her sails. They had turned east, and Worsley did his best to keep them on course for South Georgia. But the boat pitched and rolled violently on the waves. The Skipper needed two men steadying him on either side to free up his hands for the instruments. Even then, he found it impossible to line up his sextant accurately with the sun. He figured they'd made 128 miles so far. But he wasn't at all sure he could find an island 700 miles away.

As they fought their way through the giant swells, the men took four-hour watches in groups of three. The sailors on duty took turns steering and pumping seawater out of the hold.

For the men below there was no escape from the water. It sprayed into the hatch near the stern. It trickled through the seams in the canvas. As fast as they could pump it out it pooled in the cracks between the supplies and the ballast. It soaked underwear and socks, boots and mittens, sweaters and sleeping bags. When the men went below for their four hours' rest, their bags had frozen solid. All they could do was crawl inside and wait for their body heat to thaw the skins.

On the 28th, McNish took off his boots and socks to find his feet swollen and stark white. Frostbite had set in, and Vincent had it even worse. He was already having trouble moving around. They had made 146 miles by Worsley's reckoning—650 to go.

Shackleton kept a close eye on the men. When someone looked to be struggling, he noticed. But instead of singling the poor sailor out, he simply ordered an extra ration of hot milk or a biscuit for everyone.

Food, however, was a chore. It took three men just to heat a pot of hoosh. One man held the oil-burning camp stove; the other two protected it from the spray and kept the pot from overturning when the boat rocked. Every cup of hoosh came clogged with reindeer hair from the sleeping bags. The biscuits were drenched and tasted like the sea.

They made 92 miles the fifth day and 78 the sixth. At times the swells rose so high that when they rode into the troughs the wind died and their sails slackened. If the men looked sideways, it seemed they were riding in a tunnel made of water.

The temperature plummeted the night of April 30, and they woke around 3 a.m. to find the boat riding dangerously low in the water. Shackleton and Worsley stood up in the hatch and discovered the reason. A thick sheet of ice coated the entire deck, and the extra weight was slowly sinking the *Caird*.

One by one in the pitch dark, the men climbed onto the deck to hack away at the ice. The wind whipped and the boat lurched under their feet. They fought to keep their balance on the sheer surface. Every five minutes, one man would crawl back, exhausted and fingers frozen. Another would take his place.

At one point the boat lurched and Vincent, whose frostbitten feet would barely support him anymore, lost his footing. He slid toward the edge of the boat. Worsley leaned over to grab his hand but missed. Vincent managed to clutch the mast just before he went overboard into the Drake Passage.

Worsley took Vincent's place and breathed a sigh of relief. He found it less stressful to be out on the deck himself than to watch the others, knowing that with one slip he might have to sit helpless while a boatmate disappeared into the frigid ocean.

Two hours later, the *Caird* still had six passengers. Once again she rode high enough in the water for the men to relax. They retired below for a cup of hair-infested hoosh. That day and the next they would have to perform the de-icing ritual again.

Just after noon on May 2, a wandering albatross soared in on a southwest wind. It swept down to within 10 feet of the *Caird*. Its wings, built for long-distance flight, stretched nearly half the length of the boat. The bird circled the men for hours, filling them with envy. Worsley figured it could fly Elephant Island to South Georgia, hundreds of feet above the bone-chilling spray, in 15 hours.

They had been at sea for eight days. They were not yet halfway there.

------◆------

Back on Elephant Island, the men rallied after the blizzard swamped their hut. With Wild's encouragement, they

Two albatross fly over the Drake Passage.

patched the holes in the walls and brought in a blubber stove to warm the cramped space. Someone decided to call their home the "Snuggery." It became a haven from the wind, the sleet, and the snow.

During the day, the men arranged crates around the Snuggery so they could sit for meals. Over hoosh or penguin steak they debated the date of their liberation. Guesses ranged from May 12 to June 1. Lees was among the few willing to disagree out loud. He was convinced they would have to winter on the island. Even if the *Caird* made it to South Georgia, he thought, the pack would close and the Boss wouldn't make it back until spring.

Finally, after two weeks of brutal weather, May 2 brought a welcome sight: the sun. "This is the first time we have seen it since reaching the God forsaken spot," Lees wrote. By midmorning a display of soggy sleeping bags and clothes lay around the camp, drying in the air.

———◈———

By their tenth day at sea, the men on the *Caird* had been enjoying the sun for two full days. During the day the boat looked like the camp at Cape Wild, sleeping bags and clothes draped over the deck to dry. "We manage to get most of our gear into a pleasantly moderate state of dampness," wrote Worsley.

That was about all they could hope for. And the sun hadn't made any real improvement in their condition. No one on board could feel his feet anymore. Without any room for exercise, all they could do was sit and wiggle their toes, hoping they wouldn't get any worse. Their hands were raw and blistered from frostbite. Knees were scraped and bleeding from crawling among the rocks in the keel. Nasty boils from the saltwater rose on their wrists, ankles, and backsides.

They'd been making 30 to 50 miles a day for several days. As they made their way through a relatively calm sea on May 4, Crean noticed they had finished one cask of drinking water. He tapped into the second and last cask and took a drink. To his horror, it was only half full and tasted salty. He immediately thought back to the day they left. As they were loading the *Caird*, one of the casks had been dropped overboard. Crean realized that it must have been punctured on the rocks.

South Georgia still lay 300 miles to the east, and the only water they had left was contaminated with salt. Drinking it could dehydrate them faster than not drinking at all.

Crean called Shackleton down from the deck to give him the news. The Boss, feeling the strain of the voyage, snapped at his loyal second officer. Obviously they had no choice, he said; they would have to drink it anyway.

They made more than 150 miles the next two days. But everyone grew weaker by the day. On May 6, Shackleton cut the daily water ration to half a cup. Vincent grew sullen and dejected. McNish had stopped writing in his diary. The men sometimes begged for an extra drink, but the Boss refused to bend. If Worsley's reckoning could be trusted, they should see land in two days. But if the wind shifted they could spend another week on the boat, and they couldn't afford to exhaust their supplies.

The next day, the boat lurched on unpredictable seas. Worsley tried several times to calculate their position. He told Shackleton he could be at least 10 miles off. They had been planning to aim for the northwestern tip of South Georgia and sail around the north edge to one of the whaling stations in Stromness Bay. Now, Shackleton didn't want to risk missing the island to the north. If they did, there would be nothing but 3,000 miles of ocean between them and the African coast. Instead, they decided to make for the broad southwestern shore. That would put them on the other side of the island from the whaling stations. But at least they would be standing on dry ground.

———◆———

On May 9, 200 Gentoo penguins popped up from the ocean onto the dry ground at Cape Wild. The men had been killing penguins since they arrived, and they had it down to a system. They would chase the 2-foot-tall birds up the sloping side of the glacier. Lees would then climb up and herd seven or eight of them down at a time, where they were met by a mob of salivating, bearded men with clubs and axes.

On this day, Lees had made the climb six or seven times when Wild called off the hunt. Fifty penguins was enough for the day, Wild said.

The storekeeper was livid. Two men could go through meat from a penguin in a single meal. At this point they had six weeks' worth of seal meat. They were eating the penguin meat as fast as they butchered it. Why wasn't Wild taking every opportunity to stock up for the winter?

The next day, Hurley arranged 20 bearded, grim-faced men in front of the Snuggery for a picture. They were a sorry-looking lot. Wordie was nursing an infected hand. Rickinson was recovering from his heart attack and had a giant boil on his backside from the boat journey. Greenstreet was still hobbled from frostbite. Blackborow, whose feet were beginning to turn black, didn't make it out of the hut for the photograph. Hudson hadn't been out of his sleeping bag much at all. No one knew exactly what was wrong with him, but they described his condition as a "nervous breakdown."

They were "the most motley and unkempt assembly that ever was projected on a plate," Hurley thought. "All looking forward to the relief which we earnestly hope to be here in a few days."

———◆———

On May 8, their "relief" woke to choppy seas and a thick mist. The crew of the *Caird* ate breakfast quickly so they could go on deck to look for land. They had made good time the day before, and Worsley figured they were getting close. The mist gave way to tantalizing breaks of sun. Then the sky closed again and they couldn't see a thing. Could it be that Worsley's calculations had been wrong all along? Had they missed South Georgia and were now headed out to sea?

Then, just after 10:30 a.m., Vincent saw a clump of seaweed floating in the surf. Not long after, a cormorant appeared in the sky above the boat. As all sailors knew, cormorants rarely stray more than 15 miles from land.

The fog lifted again just after noon, and the men heard McCarthy call out, "Land!" Sure enough, to the northeast, a black cliff rose from the sea, spotted with patches of snow. It couldn't have been more than 10 miles off, but clouds moved in and cut it off from view.

Shackleton said simply, "We've done it."

No one responded. They stared toward the horizon, as if needing another glimpse before they were convinced it was true. In a minute or two the clouds parted again and the land reappeared. Now they could make out grass on the hillside—the first vegetation they'd seen since they left the very same island in December 1914.

The *Caird* touched the shore at 5 p.m. two days later. She'd been battered by hurricane force winds on the way in, and for a time it seemed as though she would be smashed against the land they'd been dreaming of for two weeks.

The artist Marston's drawing of the *Caird*, battling a hurricane to get to shore on South Georgia.

Now, she floated in the calm waters of South Georgia's King Haakon Bay.

Shackleton jumped into 3 feet of water and dragged her toward the beach. Three others jumped out and held the boat against the pull of the surf while Shackleton fixed the rope around a rock.

They all came ashore and stood as best they could on shaky legs. To the side, someone noticed a small stream of clear, cold water, running to the sea. In an instant, six men were on their knees, funneling water into their mouths with cupped hands.

Above the kneeling men rose a line of craggy, snow-covered peaks. Thirty miles beyond the mountains, on the northeast coast of the island, lay the only human settlements within 950 miles. No one had ever set foot more than a mile inland on South Georgia. But the six men couldn't think about that now. At the moment, they were just grateful to be alive—and back on solid ground.

CHAPTER 13

OVER THE MOUNTAINS

At 2 a.m. on May 19 Shackleton, Worsley, and Crean climbed out of their sleeping bags and into the cold morning air of King Haakon Bay. They made a pot of hoosh and devoured it. By the light of a full moon they gathered a 50-foot length of rope, an ice ax, a compass, and binoculars. They shoved three days' worth of sledding rations and biscuits into socks. They picked up a small pot, a box of 48 matches, and the oil-burning stove with enough fuel for six hot meals. Shouldering the socks and the rest of their equipment, they headed east along the beach.

The men picked their way across the foot of a glacier, with the surf lapping at their feet. Then they turned inland up a long, snow-covered slope in the general direction of the whaling stations at Stromness Bay. In their path lay an obstacle course of 6,000-foot peaks and valleys filled with glacier ice. The whalers Shackleton had spoken to in the past assumed it was land that no one could cross. Then again, no one had ever needed to.

Shackleton, Worsley, and Crean had no choice. The *Caird* had been battered on her way into King Haakon Bay, and no one thought she could stand a 150-mile journey around South Georgia to Stromness Bay. The overland route was the only option. Worsley figured it was 17 miles in a straight line. But the rugged terrain would force them onto a much longer path.

Since they beached the *Caird*, the men had spent the last week gathering strength. They feasted on albatross and elephant seal. But even after they'd consumed all the clean water and hot food they could, Vincent and McNish were in no shape to travel. They would stay behind with McCarthy.

With the moonlight guiding them, Shackleton, Worsley, and Crean trudged up the slope, sinking shin-deep in snow. They roped themselves together for safety. Shackleton broke trail, Crean followed, and Worsley brought up the rear. The Skipper checked his compass and called out "Starboard!" "Port!" or "Steady!" as though they were still aboard a ship.

To the east lay a range of peaks silhouetted against the sky like the fingers of a hand. Between the fingers the ridgeline dropped into high passes. Through one of those passes, Worsley figured, lay a route to Stromness Bay.

When the three men reached the foot of the range, they had no idea which pass would give them the easiest path. Twice they trudged up the mountainside, carving steps in the ice when the slope got too steep. Twice they peered over the edge of a pass to find a sharp slope that dropped off into a 1,500-foot cliff a few yards away.

By the time they reached the third pass it was late afternoon. They sat atop a ridge so sharp they could straddle

Probable route of the famous impromptu toboggan ride in 1916

Crean Glacier

Antarctic Bay

The path to the whaling station, with the "fingers" of the Trident Ridge in the background.

it. The light was slipping away. A dense fog crept up the mountain range on either side. They could barely see the slope below them. It looked more gradual than the last two, but no one could be sure.

Shackleton decided they had to risk it. The ridge stood at about 4,500 feet. If they got caught at this elevation at night without sleeping bags, they could easily freeze to death.

Still roped together, they made their way down, the Boss hacking steps into the slope. A half hour later they had descended 100 yards at best. With darkness closing in, Shackleton carved out a ledge big enough for the three of them and peered down the slope. It seemed to be flattening out, but it vanished in the fog before they could see the bottom. There was no way to be certain it didn't fall off into a sheer cliff.

Shackleton told the men they had to speed up their descent, no matter the risk—and he knew exactly how. At the Boss's instruction, each man looped his section of rope into a coil. Worsley sat on his coil and linked his legs and arms around Shackleton in front of him. Crean did the same behind Worsley. Then, with the fate of 28 men resting in their laps, they launched themselves into the fog.

On May 19, as the three men careened down a mountainside on South Georgia, pack ice moved in and choked Cape Wild. For weeks, the Elephant Island party had been watching the wind the way they had at Patience Camp. When it blew from the south, the pack ice loosened. Penguins gained access to their beach, oblivious to what lay in store for them. When the wind blew hard from the north, the ice moved in. Their food supply vanished—and so did any path a relief ship might follow to the shore of Cape Wild.

But no matter how icebound the cape became, Wild woke the men every morning with the same hopeful greeting: "Lash up and stow! The boss may come today." In a few minutes, sleeping bags were rolled and ready to go—not that any of the men ever wanted to see the inside of one again.

The entire day revolved around meals—supplying food for them, preparing them, eating them, and talking about them. At 9:30 a.m. they sat around the stove for a breakfast of fried penguin breast. Wild assigned tasks for the day: There might be mending to do on the Snuggery, but mostly they hunted, skinned, and butchered penguins. They ate hoosh at 12:30 p.m. and hoosh again at 4:30 p.m. At night Hussey often played banjo while some of the men

Gentoo penguins, about to be added to the meager food supply on Cape Wild.

sang. By 7 p.m. they were in their sleeping bags and they didn't come out for 14 hours.

As winter closed in, Lees's anxiety grew. Seals were few and far between. And if the pack clogged the cape for good, penguins would probably vanish too. In the middle of May they ran out of seal blubber to fuel the fire and started burning penguin skins. The stove consumed 20 or 25 of them a day, and on May 15 they had enough for just two weeks.

As May wore on, Lees counted off the dwindling supplies. On May 23: "goodbye sardines." The next day: "Farewell tapioca."

Fewer and fewer of the men in the Snuggery were willing to bet on an early escape. "Installing ourselves for the winter, little hope being entertained of immediate relief," wrote Hurley on May 23. "It is now a month since the Caird's departure."

But most of the men shared Macklin's reluctance to give up hope. Every morning, even when pack ice clogged the ocean as far as the eye could see, the doctor climbed to the highest point on Cape Wild and scanned the water for a sail. "In spite of everything," he wrote, "I cannot help hoping to see a ship coming along to our relief."

When Shackleton, Worsley, and Crean pushed off the lonely South Georgia ridge on their improvised sled, Worsley was terrified. Snow lashed at their faces as they hurtled through the darkness. At any moment the ground could disappear beneath them, and they would plummet a thousand feet to their deaths. The months of cold and starvation, the mind-numbing hours in the tents, the harrowing boat journeys through the ice—all of it would come to nothing.

Then, as they gathered speed and the mountain rushed past, Worsley suddenly realized he was grinning. Maybe it was delirium from lack of food and water. Maybe it was months of tension finally breaking loose. But before long all three men were yelling into the wind like they were out for a toboggan ride on Christmas Day.

After a minute or two the slope began to flatten out. They slowed and came to a stop in a snowbank. The men stood up and looked at one another. In the strangely formal gesture they used to mark the milestones of their survival, they shook hands.

Then they looked back up the slope. No one knew how far they had slid. Shackleton, who was not given to exaggeration, figured 900 feet. The more colorful Worsley would later claim 3,000.

Finally, Shackleton said, "It's not good to do that kind of thing too often."

They had two more slopes to climb, and it took them all night. But in the first glimmer of daylight they stood at the top of a ridge. They could see the tortured rock formations of Stromness Bay below. A short while later, the throaty sound of a steam whistle rose from the bay below. It was 7 a.m., and the whistle was calling the whalers to work. It was the first sound of civilization the men had heard since they left the island on December 5, 1914.

Seven hours later they stumbled into the Husvik whaling station in Stromness Bay, not far from Grytviken, where they had stayed before setting out 17 months ago. The familiar stench of decomposing whale hung in the air. They paused for a moment, suddenly self-conscious. They hadn't bathed in more than half a year. Their beards were long, their clothes tattered and stained. Worsley surprised Shackleton by producing a couple of safety pins from his pocket. He made some hasty repairs to his pants that only called attention to the mess.

The first people they saw were a couple of boys, 10 or 12 years old. Shackleton asked them how to get to the station manager's house. The boys took one look at the strangers and ran.

Finally, the three survivors stood facing the station manager, who had hosted them briefly during their month on South Georgia in 1914. Now, the man stared at them blankly.

"Don't you know me?" Shackleton asked.

"I know your voice; you're the mate of the *Daisy*," the station manager said, confusing him with someone else.

The response came, quiet and matter-of-fact: "My name is Shackleton."

CHAPTER 14

LAST STAND

On Tuesday morning, May 23, the steam whistle that had welcomed Shackleton, Worsley, and Crean to Stromness Bay three days earlier sounded again. This time it blew a farewell to the three men, who stood on the deck of a whaler called the *Southern Sky*. They steamed out of the bay and turned west for Elephant Island.

Three days was not a lot of recovery time, but Shackleton felt he couldn't wait any longer. The coldest days of winter had nearly arrived. The pack would be closing soon—if it hadn't already.

During their time on South Georgia, the men had been bathed, shaved, and fed. They had told their story to a host of astonished whalers. They also retrieved McNish, McCarthy, and Vincent from King Haakon Bay and arranged to have them sent back to England. Seeing

McNish without layers of bulky sweaters and jackets, Shackleton realized how emaciated the carpenter was. Their rescue had come just in time.

As the *Southern Sky* motored through the Drake Passage, Shackleton started to worry. On the third night out, the temperature dropped and a thin coat of ice formed around the ship. They veered north to avoid the pack, and then steered south for Elephant Island. When ice blocked their way they ventured farther west and tried again. The pack ice that had closed in on Cape Wild in the middle of May still surrounded the island.

Recognizing that the *Southern Sky* wasn't built for battle with the pack, Shackleton gave in and retreated north to the Falkland Islands. He had been stopped 70 miles from Elephant Island, no closer than he had been when they had launched their boats from Patience Camp.

In the Falklands, Shackleton searched desperately for another ship. He cabled the British navy, and word came back that they couldn't send a ship until October.

Shackleton had assumed that the war would be a thing of the past. In fact, battles were still raging around the world. The young men of Western Europe had been dug into trenches for two years, slaughtering one another. More than 10 million people had died in the war already.

It was a rude awakening for Shackleton. He had expected

a rousing welcome, but the rest of the world had other things to worry about.

All Shackleton had earned for his ordeal on the ice was a cable from the king: "Rejoice to hear of your safe arrival in the Falkland Islands and trust your comrades on Elephant Island may soon be rescued."

———◆———

On Elephant Island, Shackleton's comrades were wondering just how soon that rescue would come. "One cannot help but be a bit anxious about Sir Ernest," Lees wrote on June 7 from his perch in the Snuggery. "One wonders how he fared, where he is now and how it is that he has not yet been able to relieve us."

The most common guess from the men around the stove was that the Boss had tried to get to them in a whaler and failed. Now he was hunting for a ship that would be a match for the ice. Accurate as it was, that scenario left an important question unanswered: Would he make it before they starved to death?

The penguins came and went, providing food and fodder for the running feud between Lees and Wild. On June 8, after a few days of bloody slaughter, Wild thought they had food to last them through August. Lees insisted they would run out in July.

The slaughter: skinning penguins on Elephant Island.

On June 15, the monotony was interrupted by a grim but essential task. The flesh in Blackborow's frostbitten toes had died and turned completely black—a condition known as gangrene. Now the rot was threatening to spread up his leg. The doctors Macklin and McIlroy decided they would have to amputate the toes on Blackborow's left foot.

Wild ordered everyone out of the Snuggery except Hudson and Greenstreet, who couldn't walk. The doctors stripped to their undershirts. Hurley tended the fire while Wild boiled the surgical instruments in a hoosh pot to sterilize them. Macklin held a cloth soaked in chloroform over Blackborow's face until the patient dropped off to sleep. Hudson, still bedridden, turned away. Greenstreet followed the whole procedure, fascinated. When Macklin cut the toes off Blackborow's foot they dropped with a frozen clatter into a tin can below.

After three hours the medical team emerged from the hut. The rest of the men had huddled in a cave and cut each other's hair to pass the time. Cold, hungry, and bored, they filed back into the Snuggery to find the patient sleeping peacefully.

By the beginning of June, the men on Elephant Island had been waiting for nearly two months. Wild had stopped the charade of rolling up the bags in the morning. He insisted that everyone except the invalids get an hour of exercise each day. But there wasn't much work to do. Sometimes the men stayed in their sleeping bags nearly the entire day. Macklin noted on July 6 that he could lie for hours on end "without even so much as thinking."

Greenstreet summed it up even more vividly one night: "Everyone spent the day rotting in their bags with blubber and tobacco smoke—so passes another rotten day."

———◆———

On Saturday, July 22, while the men in the Snuggery toasted their loved ones, Shackleton anchored for the night in an Argentine schooner, 100 miles away. It was his third attempt to reach Elephant Island. A month earlier he had come within a few miles of Cape Wild before the ice nearly destroyed his ship.

Now, Worsley once again tried to carve his way through the pack. But the schooner was half the size of the *Endurance*. She was pushed around by slabs of ice heavier than the ship. Worsley couldn't get them anywhere near Cape Wild.

At the beginning of August, exactly two years after the *Endurance* left London, Shackleton gave up again. He and Worsley fought their way through a gale back to the Falklands, knowing they were running out of options. By this time, for all they knew, half the crew could be dead. Shackleton could no longer talk about the men he'd left behind without growing sullen and testy. Worsley noticed that the Boss's hair had turned gray since they left England.

On August 6, just after the schooner turned her stern to Elephant Island and headed north, Frank Hurley stood on a rise the men called Lookout Bluff. Temperatures had started to climb above freezing the last week. The sun shone bright on the ocean. A number of men joined Hurley, warming themselves on the rocks. Beyond their little inlet, a few icebergs absorbed a pounding from the Cape Horn rollers. Aside from the bergs, the sea was clear of ice, as far as the eye could see. "It would be ideal weather for the ship to arrive," Hurley concluded.

Even as it seemed more and more unlikely, rescue was still everyone's fantasy. The Snuggery had become intolerable. On warm days, snowmelt seeped in from all corners. The floor turned into a soupy mess of rotting seal bits, reindeer hairs, and penguin guano. At one point Lees found a pool of penguin blood under his sleeping bag and half a pound of rancid meat stuck between the stones. They had started referring to their home as the "sty."

Blackborow, who had barely left the hut in four months, had the worst of it. His foot wasn't healing well, and the doctors were worried about infection. The young stowaway was in a lot of pain, but he never complained. The engineer Alfred Kerr had appointed himself Blackborow's personal nurse. On August 12, he sewed a few transparent photo coverings into the wall of the tent so Blackborow could have some light.

By mid-August the food supply was dwindling, and Lees wasn't the only one worried anymore. They were nearly out of penguin breast so they boiled the skinny legs and ate them for breakfast. On August 20, the nut food supply gave out, casting everyone into a deep depression. A few days later they were stewing penguin carcasses and seal bones to make broth. They boiled seaweed into a jelly and ate it. The men spent hours scouring the rocks in shallow water for limpets, shellfish that are so tiny it took hundreds to make a meal.

On August 29, they had seen exactly 6 penguins in 2 days—enough to feed a single breakfast to 12 men. They had 5 days' worth of food left, and the men were openly worrying about Shackleton. Even Wild admitted the Boss and the rest of the *Caird*'s crew might well have been swamped in the Drake Passage and lost forever.

That day, Wild announced to a few of the men that he had made up his mind. At the beginning of October he would take the *Docker* from the Snuggery and patch it up as best he could. With a crew of four men, he would launch for Deception Island.

The plan was a long shot. They'd be running against the wind, and all they had for a mainsail were tattered pieces of tent canvas. As for the men left behind, they were already packed like sardines into their hut. With the *Docker* gone their space would be cut in half.

But when he sat with his diary that night, Lees felt like Deception Island was probably their only hope. "The idea of a ship ever coming now," he wrote, "is getting more and more remote."

The next day, a clear, cold dawn gave way to gloomy skies by late morning. Several feet of wet snow had accumulated around the Snuggery in the last two weeks. The men spent the morning shoveling and catching limpets. At around 1 p.m., they were sitting around the hut eating a hoosh made from seal backbone when they heard Marston's voice outside. "Wild, there's a ship! Shall we light a fire?"

Twenty men, who had been hungry and listless a moment before, suddenly sprang to life. Mugs full of precious hoosh dropped to the ground. The entire crew tried to exit the tent at once. In seconds the wall had been torn to shreds, and a crowd of bony, bearded castaways hobbled down the slope to the shore. Even Hudson roused himself from his sick bed. He and Lees carried Blackborow out and sat him down where he could watch the excitement.

The ship was still a mile off, and everyone took a long look to make sure that it wasn't an iceberg. They had been fooled before and couldn't tolerate it happening again.

She was unmistakably a ship—but it wasn't clear what kind. She wasn't a whaler or an ice-breaker but some kind of steam tug. The men thought maybe she had arrived by accident, but they didn't care, as long as she didn't leave without them.

Hurley made a pile of seal blubber and dry grass and doused it with kerosene. It exploded in flames when he put a match to it, but failed to produce much smoke.

Macklin ran to an oar they had dug into the snow and hoisted his jacket as high as it would go.

Neither effort was especially effective, but at this point it didn't matter. The ship was fast approaching, until she anchored 150 yards from shore. The men still couldn't tell if Shackleton was aboard.

Finally, the ship lowered a lifeboat, and a sturdy figure climbed down into it. The men let out as loud a cheer as they could manage. As the boat approached, Shackleton called out, "Are you all well?"

"We are all well, Boss," Wild yelled back.

"Thank God," Shackleton said.

He stepped off the boat into the crowd of grateful men. Perhaps proud of the fact that they had survived four months on their own, the men begged Shackleton to come see the Snuggery.

The Boss refused. He was already looking anxiously out to sea for signs of their old enemy, the pack. In an hour, he had all 22 men and their meager possessions aboard the ship. Worsley pointed them north for Argentina.

There was no ice in sight.

Going home: A boatload of castaways leaves Elephant Island behind, with Shackleton's ship, a Chilean vessel called the *Yelcho*, waiting in the background.

COMING HOME

At 7 a.m. on October 8, 1916, the crew of the *Endurance* gathered one final time at the railway station in Buenos Aires, Argentina. Shackleton and Worsley were leaving for a ship that would take them to the other side of Antarctica. The Ross Sea party—the men who laid supplies for the overland trek that never happened— had been trapped on the ice for nearly two years and needed rescue.

The men at the railway station had been ashore for a month and they were beginning to look like human beings again. Their clothes were clean. A year's worth of stove soot and penguin grease had been scrubbed and scraped from their skin. They'd been shaved, clipped, and snipped by a barber.

But no amount of grooming could erase the effects of their ordeal. Blackborow had been willing to do almost anything to join the expedition. Now he was in the hospital recovering from the emergency amputation of his toes. Thomas McLeod was just starting to gain back the 100 pounds he had lost.

The men had been crammed together in close quarters for two years, and yet they had trouble saying good-bye. Both the Boss and the Skipper felt depressed to be leaving the others behind. The old seaman McLeod wept when he said good-bye to William Bakewell. And Bakewell felt just as sad. "I had to say goodbye to the finest group of men that it has ever been my good fortune to be with," he recalled later.

The crew in Chile on September 3, 1916, still unshaved and unwashed.

A train pulled up. Shackleton and Worsley stepped inside and they were gone. How easy this journey must have seemed after 18 months spent paying for every mile in blood and sweat, aching limbs and frostbitten fingers.

———◆———

For most of the men, the return to Europe was a shock. They had been through the most grueling experience of their lives. The rest of the world was trapped in its own brutal hell.

The *Endurance* had left England during the first week of World War I. Since then, millions of people had died on the battlefields of Europe, Africa, and the Middle East. It was the bloodiest war Europe had ever seen, and the crew of the *Endurance* had missed it all. "We were like men arisen from the dead to a world gone mad," wrote Shackleton.

That world didn't exactly give the men a hero's welcome. Barely a village in England had gotten by without losing a good portion of its young men in battle. Those men had made the ultimate sacrifice, and even though the crew of the *Endurance* had been through hell, they had survived. When Shackleton returned from one of his attempts to rescue the Elephant Island crew, a newspaper reporter overheard someone on the docks grumbling about what a waste the expedition had been. "'E ought ter 'ave been at the war long ago instead of messing about on icebergs," the man complained.

At least some of the men took that criticism to heart. They felt ashamed they had missed so much of the war. Nearly all of them enlisted in the military as soon as they could. Most made it through to the end. Tim McCarthy, who had survived an open-boat voyage across the worst seas in the world, was killed at sea by enemy fire six weeks after he signed up. Alf Cheetham, third officer on the *Endurance*, went down with his ship in the North Sea less than two months before the war ended.

———◆———

By war's end, Shackleton had found his way back to the snow and ice. He was directing the transport of troops and supplies in northern Russia. Now, he had to think about making a living again. And that meant telling the story of the *Endurance* to whoever would pay to listen.

Reliving the ordeal on the ice wasn't easy for Shackleton. Before he left for the war, he had dictated much of the story to an author he hired to help him write a book. Shackleton had to stop and leave the room to compose himself during the retelling. After the first half hour, he turned to his longtime friend and adviser Leonard Tripp, who was sitting in on the sessions. Fighting back tears, he said, "Tripp, you don't know what I've been through, and I'm going through it all over again, and I can't do it."

But Shackleton did do it, because he needed the money. He traveled through England showing Hurley's slides and telling the story to half-full rooms. The experience wore him down. Night after night he recounted the details—the diet of blubber and bannocks, the shooting of the dogs, the desperate boat journeys. All the while the images flickered behind him like a bad dream—the *Endurance* crushed to death in the ice a thousand times over. Before long Shackleton was drinking heavily and wracked with colds, fevers, and back pain.

Three years back at home had brought him to a familiar place: It was time for another expedition.

Shackleton hatched a vague plan to sail around the entire Antarctic continent. But the real goal was simply to get away from civilization again. He didn't have the patience for bills and cocktail parties. "I am just good as an explorer and nothing else," he had written to his wife before leaving in the *Endurance*.

Or as Reginald James the physicist put it, "Shackleton afloat was a more likeable character than Shackleton ashore."

On September 17, 1921, Shackleton left England in the 111-foot, oak-framed ship *Quest*. Many of the *Endurance* crew had vowed never to go back to the Antarctic. But Macklin, Worsley, McIlroy, Wild, Hussey, McLeod, the engineer Alfred Kerr, and the cook Charles Green were all on board.

From the start of the voyage, it was obvious Shackleton wasn't healthy. He looked pale and haggard. His plans were unclear. They were headed for South Georgia, but beyond that no one knew exactly where they were going.

Every time the doctor Macklin asked about Shackleton's health, the Boss changed the subject. All he wanted to do was sit and listen to Hussey play the banjo—just as they had done during the endless days on the ice. Macklin had trouble explaining to the new crew members what was so inspiring about the man who had engineered the greatest escape in the history of polar exploration.

On January 4, 1922, the snow-covered crags of South Georgia edged into view, and Shackleton came to life. He and Worsley grabbed anyone who would listen and pointed out the landmarks of their last-ditch trek across the island. There in the distance was the ridge on which they'd coiled their ropes and slid into the unknown. And there was the exact point where they had emerged from the mountains. The elation they had felt five and half years ago all came rushing back. Worsley said he and Shackleton turned into "a pair of excitable kids."

Fridjof Jacobsen, the station manager who had treated the officers of the *Endurance* to whale steaks before they sailed into the ice, came out to greet the men. Once again, they ate dinner ashore. Back in his cabin on board the *Quest*, Shackleton told his diary it had been "a wonderful evening." For the first time since the voyage began, the Boss seemed like himself again.

That night, in the early hours of the morning, Macklin was called to Shackleton's bedside. The Boss had been stricken by a heart attack. He asked Macklin feebly what the doctor was going to ask him to give up this time: smoking? drinking?

A few minutes later, Shackleton was dead.

———◆———

Frank Wild took command of the *Quest* and sailed without much purpose for a few more months. Before he headed home to England, he navigated past Elephant Island. The men squinted over the side of the ship at the windbeaten shore where Shackleton had rescued them from near certain death.

That night, Macklin sat down to write in his journal. "Ah what memories what memories!—they rush to one like a great flood & bring tears to ones eyes. . . Once more

I see the little boat, Frankie Wild's hut, dark & dirty, but a snug little shelter all the same. Once more I see the old faces & hear the old voices—old friends scattered everywhere. But to express all I feel is impossible."

The *Quest* turned and sailed for home. Behind them, Shackleton lay buried under the snow on South Georgia with the stench of rotting whale in the air. It was exactly what he would have wanted. Before the *Quest* left England, he had told a friend that he didn't want to die in Europe. He said, "I shall go on going till one day I shall not come back."

GLOSSARY

ballast: heavy material placed in a boat to make it more stable in the water

bilge: lowest part of a ship where water collects

bo'sun: an abbreviation for boatswain, the sailor in charge of most work on deck

chanties: songs sung by sailors, often in rhythm with their work

dirge: a slow, mournful piece of music

floe: a large sheet of floating ice

fugue: a piece of music with one interwoven theme played by different instruments

growler: a floating chunk of ice, broken free from an iceberg

gunwales (pronounced gunnels): the top edge of a ship's sidewalls

mutiny: deliberate revolt against officers in the military or on board a ship

port: the left side of a ship when you're facing forward

scurvy: disease that terrorized explorers for centuries, caused by a lack of vitamin C in the diet

skua: seabird that scavenges for food by stealing fish from other birds

snow petrel: white seabird that feeds on fish and dead animals

spar: strong pole used to support lines or sails on a ship

starboard: the right side of a ship when you're facing forward

stern: the rear of a ship

stoker: sailors whose job it is to throw fuel into the boiler that powers a ship's steam engine

AUTHOR'S NOTE

Antarctica is unusual in the history of exploration because the people who risked their lives there knew they wouldn't get much in return—nothing that would make them rich, anyway. In all its 5.4 million square miles, Antarctica had not a single acre of fertile soil. If the ground harbored gold or silver, it was buried under thousands of feet of snow and ice.

The fact that Antarctica had little of practical value to offer to visitors makes its story a happy one compared to the rest of the world. In the Americas and in Australia, European explorers created new nations but left a trail of destruction in their wake. In the years after Europeans arrived, close to 90 percent of the American and Australian indigenous population died, either in battle or from diseases carried across the ocean by the newcomers. On the west coast of Africa, slave traders captured or bought more than

12 million human beings and transported them to the Americas. For 350 years, black men and women worked and died in slavery from the sugar plantations of Brazil to the tobacco fields of Virginia.

In Antarctica, however, the entire continent survived almost unchanged. It was uninhabited by humans when the first European explorers arrived, so there was no one to befriend, conquer, or enslave. No one could settle there. Hunters went after whales and fur seals with a vengeance. But for most of the last 50 years, hunting has been outlawed. The Antarctic whale and fur seal populations are recovering.

Today Antarctica is the one large piece of land on Earth that has barely been touched by humans. About 5,000 people stay there during the summer. That's one resident for every 1,080 square miles. During the winter, the population drops to 1,000.

Nearly all of Antarctica's residents are there for one reason: to do scientific research. More than 50 countries have signed a treaty agreeing that no single nation can claim to own the continent. The treaty bans all military activity and mining.

Thanks in part to the international agreement, Antarctica is one of the least polluted places on Earth. There are no landfills there. All trash has to be burned, recycled, or carried back to civilization. Antarctic waters are free of the toxic runoff that has created low-oxygen "dead zones" in other ocean regions.

Unfortunately, that's not the full story. Antarctica may not have much of a human presence on its shores, but in today's world, no place on Earth can stay fully isolated from human activity.

As we burn fossil fuels to run factories, cars, and power plants, we pump methane and carbon dioxide gas into the atmosphere. Those gases act like a greenhouse around the planet. They trap heat from the sun close to the Earth.

As the gases build up, our climate warms, and Antarctica is already feeling the effects.

The entire continent is surrounded by floating ice shelves—the barrier ice that the *Endurance* encountered as it got close to Vahsel Bay. Scientists now think warm water is drifting in from the north and melting the ice shelves from below. In July 2017, an iceberg the size of Delaware broke off the Larsen C ice shelf, about 250 miles south of Paulet Island. In that area, near the tip of the Antarctic Peninsula, temperatures have warmed by about 5 degrees in the last 70 years.

All of this may sound like good news if you're planning a visit to Antarctica. And it may, in fact, make a journey through the Weddell Sea less treacherous than it was for the crew of the *Endurance*.

But for the rest of the planet, melting ice means trouble, because when ice turns to water it drains into the sea. Some scientists predict that melting in Antarctica alone could cause sea levels to rise 3 feet in the next century. Eventually, many experts think, all the ice in Antarctica will disappear. It will happen slowly over hundreds, maybe thousands of years. But as it does, coastal areas all around the world will flood. New York, Miami, London, Amsterdam, Beijing, Venice, and Tokyo will be underwater.

The men aboard the *Endurance* were humbled by the size and power of the frozen world around them. Macklin and Lees used almost identical language to describe how the landscape made them feel—like "puny mortals" overwhelmed by the "colossal forces of nature."

Something about that experience felt larger and more authentic than the world of meetings and bosses and social obligations that awaited them at home. On Christmas 1915, Lees wrote in his diary, "Were it not for a little natural anxiety as to our ultimate progress I have never been happier in my life than I am now, for is not this kind of existence the 'real thing,' the thing I have for years set my heart on."

Maybe it was that longing that drew these men to a world that offered them tremendous risk without much material reward. They wanted to feel dwarfed by icebergs and humbled by the wind. It was a world they couldn't tame. They just hoped to prove they were worthy of it for a while.

Now, the ice that nearly killed them is in danger from the civilization they tried to leave behind. I wonder how that would make them feel.

SOURCES

Books

Alexander, Caroline. *The* Endurance: *Shackleton's Legendary Antarctic Expedition.* New York: Alfred A. Knopf, 1998.

Anthony, Jason C. *Hoosh: Roast Penguin, Scurvy Day, and Other Stories of Antarctic Cuisine.* Lincoln: University of Nebraska Press, 2012.

Bickel, Lennard. *Shackleton's Forgotten Men: The Untold Tragedy of the* Endurance *Epic.* New York: Thunder's Mouth Press, 2001.

Brooke-Hitching, Edward. *The Phantom Atlas: The Greatest Myths, Lies and Blunders on Maps.* London: Simon and Schuster, 2016.

Cherry-Garrard, Apsley. (2004). *The Worst Journey in the World*. Urbana, Illinois: Project Gutenberg. April 16, 2018, from www.gutenberg.org/ebooks /14363.

Day, David. *Antarctica: A Biography*. Oxford: Oxford University Press, 2013.

Fisher, Margery, and James Fisher. *Shackleton*. London: Barrie Books, 1957.

Fleming, Fergus. *Off the Map: Tales of Endurance and Exploration*. New York: Grove Press, 2006.

Fothergill, Alastair. *Life in the Freezer: A Natural History of the Antarctic*. London: BBC Books, 1993.

Gurney, Alan. *The Race to the White Continent: Voyages to the Antarctic*. New York: W. W. Norton, 2000.

Huntford, Roland. *The Last Place on Earth: Scott and Amundsen's Race to the South Pole*. New York: Random House, 1999.

———. *Shackleton*. New York: Carroll & Graf, 1998.

Hurley, Frank. *Argonauts of the South: Being a Narrative of Voyagings and Polar Seas and Adventures in the Antarctic with Sir Douglas Mawson and Sir Ernest Shackleton.* New York: G.P. Putnam's Sons, 1925.

————. *South With Endurance: Shackleton's Antarctic Expedition 1914–1917.* New York: BCL Press, 2001.

Landis, Marilyn J. *Antarctica: Exploring the Extreme: 400 Years of Adventure.* Chicago: Chicago Review Press, 2001.

Lansing, Alfred. *Endurance: Shackleton's Incredible Voyage.* New York: Carroll & Graf, 1999.

McClintock, James. *Lost Antarctica: Adventures in a Disappearing Land.* New York: St. Martin's Press, 2012.

Mills, Leif. *Frank Wild.* London: Caedmon of Whitby, 1999.

Nordenskjöld, Otto G., and Gunnar Andersson. *Antarctica, or Two Years Amongst the Ice of the South Pole.* London: Hurst and Blackett, Limited, 1905.

Riffenburgh, Beau. *Racing with Death: Douglas Mawson—Antarctic Explorer.* London: Bloomsbury, 2008.

Rosove, Michael H. *Let Heroes Speak: Antarctic Explorers, 1772–1922*. New York: Berkeley Books, 2000.

Shackleton, Ernest. *South: the* Endurance *Expedition*. London: Penguin, 2002 (orig. published 1919).

Smith, Michael. *An Unsung Hero: Tom Crean, Antarctic Survivor*. Wilton, Cork: The Collins Press, 2000.

———. *Shackleton: By Endurance We Conquer*. London: Oneworld, 2014.

———. *Sir James Wordie, Polar Crusader: Exploring the Arctic and Antarctic*. Edinburgh: Birlin, 2004.

Thomson, John. *Elephant Island and Beyond: The Life and Diaries of Thomas Orde Lees*. Norwich, Norfolk: Erskine Press, 2003.

Tyler-Lewis, Kelly. *The Lost Men: The Harrowing Saga of Shackleton's Ross Sea Party*. New York: Viking, 2006.

Walker, Gabrielle. *Antarctica: An Intimate Portrait of a Mysterious Continent*. New York: Houghton Mifflin Harcourt, 2013.

Wilford, John Noble. *The Mapmakers: The Story of the Great Pioneers in Cartography—from Antiquity to the Space Age.* New York: Alfred A. Knopf, 1981.

Worsley, F. A. *Endurance: An Epic of Polar Adventure.* (orig. published 1931.) New York: W. W. Norton, 2000.

Diaries and Journals

Hurley, Frank. Diary, 1914-1916. Transcript by Shane Murphy. MS 883, National Library of Australia.

McNish, Harry. Journal of Harry McNish, 1914-1916. Transcript by Shane Murphy. MS-1389. National Library of Australia.

Orde-Lees, Thomas. *The Diary of Thomas H. Orde-Lees.* Transcript by Margot Morrell. Rauner Stefansson Special Collections Library, Dartmouth College.

Wordie, James. "Weddell Sea Log." Reprinted in Michael Smith, *James Wordie: Polar Crusader.* Edinburgh: Birlin, 2004.

Worsley, Frank. Journal, 1914-1916. Transcript by Shane

Murphy. Micro-MS-0633. National Library of Australia.

Television

The Endurance: *Shackleton's Legendary Antarctic Expedition.* Directed by George Butler, WGBH Boston, 2000.

Articles

Hamblin, James. "How Being Cold Burns Calories." *The Atlantic*, Feb. 13, 2014. https://www.theatlantic.com /health/archive/2014/02/how-being-cold-burns -calories/283810/.

END NOTES

Prologue: Weddell Sea, Antarctica

the temperature hadn't made it above zero: Worsley diary, Oct. 26, 1915

"All hope is not given up": Hurley diary, Oct. 26, 1915

"Do you hear that?": quoted in Alexander, *The* Endurance, 88

Chapter 1: The Last Great Journey

"Mad," "Hopeless," "Possible": Tyler-Lewis, *Lost Men*, 21

"Yes, I like you": quoted in Smith, *Shackleton*, 289

"I suppose you can shout a bit": quoted in Lansing, *Endurance*, 17

land full of rivers: from the first modern world atlas, published in 1570, in Wilford, *Mapmakers*, 139

"good, honest" people: from German geographer Johannes
Schöner's 1533 *Opusculum Geographicum*, quoted in
Brooke-Hitching, *Phantom Atlas*, 225.

"doomed by Nature": from *The Journals of Captain
James Cook*, quoted in Gurney, *Race to the White
Continent*, 11

"All the money that was ever minted": quoted in Mills,
Wild, 108

"We have been beaten": from the expedition prospectus,
quoted in Alexander, *The Endurance*, 9

"Enough life and money has been spent": quoted in Smith,
Shackleton, 255

"If not required": quoted in Huntford, *Shackleton*, 379

Chapter 2: Southbound

"I think it is a good thing"; a "perfect pig": Lees diary,
Aug. 17, 1914

"It will all be put right": Lees diary, Oct. 1, 1914

"God Save the King": Worsley diary, Oct. 26, 1914

"All the troubles of the South": quoted in Smith,
Shackleton, 248

"All the strain is finished": quoted in Fisher and Fisher,
Shackleton, 331

"Do you know that on these expeditions": Wild's account

of the encounter, quoted in Hurley, *South with Endurance*, 12

"It is impossible to view this trade": Hurley diary, "An Epitome of our Stay at South Georgia, Nov. 5, 1914 to Dec. 5, 1914"

"She is breathing her last": Nordenskjöld, *Antarctica*, 536

"something which resembles the chill of death": Nordenskjöld, *Antarctica*, 290

Chapter 3: Ramming

bare land less than 2 percent of the time: for natural history of Antarctica see Fothergill, *Life in the Freezer*, 16

"I have never heard or felt": Cherry-Garrard, *Worst Journey*

"It's a splendid sensation": Worsley diary, Dec. 16, 1914

"Worsley specialized in ramming": quoted in Butler, *The Endurance*

They fought their way south: Worsley kept track daily in his diary.

"one great solid desert snowfield": Lees diary, Dec. 18, 1914

played soccer, Antarctic style: described in McNish diary, Dec. 20, 1914

"Clark! Clark!": Worsley diary, Dec. 12, 1914

The scenery, to Hurley: described in Worsley diary, Jan. 24, 1915

"Sir Ernest looks dead tired": Lees diary, Jan. 11, 1915

Shackleton named the inlet Glacier Bay: Shackleton, *South*, p. 27

"Spirits are high all round": Lees diary, Jan. 18, 1915

Chapter 4: Fast in the Ice

"No water in sight": Worsley diary, Jan. 19, 1915

"Thursday 21st . . .": McNish diary, Jan. 21-25, 1915

"I grudge every tin": Lees diary, Jan. 27, 1915

"He has an exceptionally offensive manner": Lees, Feb. 12, 1915

"Puny mortals striving frantically": Lees, Feb. 15, 1915

"I never saw such unanimous cooperation": Lees, Feb. 15, 1915

"Today . . . we practically cease being a ship": Worsley diary, Feb. 24, 1915

"We will have to wait God's will": McNish diary, Feb. 15, 1915

Chapter 5: Wintering

"A wave of depression": Wordie, "Weddell Sea Log," Jan. 29, 1915, reprinted in Smith, *Polar Crusader*, 284.

"It was an awful bloody business": Worsley diary,
   Jan. 6, 1915

"More villainous . . . looking creatures": Hurley diary,
   Feb. 10, 1915

"We are under the spell of the black Antarctic night":
   Frederick Cook, quoted in Landis, *Antarctica*, 195

"It is astounding": Hurley diary, March 6, 1915

"We have drifted 12 miles": McNish diary, June 8,
   1915

"magnificent animal": Hurley diary, April 9, 1915

"Somewhere in the crowd a pup yelps": Worsley diary,
   June 16, 1915

"She's pretty near her end": Worsley's version of the conversation, in Worsley, *Endurance*, 3–4

traffic in the streets of London: Lees quoting James, in
   Lees diary, Oct. 21, 1915

giant train with squeaking axles: Worsley diary, June
   10, 1915

"moans and groans of souls in torment": Worsley diary,
   June 10, 1915

"My birthday": McNish diary, Sept. 29, 1915

"The ship reverberates with hammers": Hurley diary,
   Oct. 12, 1915

"She seemed to say": Worsley diary, Oct. 18, 1915

"He was a cruel looking shark-like beast": Lees diary, Oct. 20, 1915

"The whole sensation": quoted in Lansing, *Endurance*, 57

"Mind you put your old diary in my bag": Lees diary, Oct. 27, 1915

"We are homeless and adrift": Hurley diary, Oct. 28, 1915

"I hope you haven't lost that cigarette case": Lees diary, Oct. 28, 1915

"for the first time in my life, we realized": Lees diary, Oct. 27, 1915

Chapter 7: "She's Gone"

"As always with him": quoted in Alexander, *The Endurance*, 94

"All are in high hopes": Hurley diary, Oct. 30, 1915

"So long as we have the bare minimum": Lees diary, Nov. 1, 1915

Unlike cold-blooded fish or reptiles: effects of cold on energy expenditure in Hamblin, "How Being Cold Burns Calories"

"All we seem to live for": quoted in Lansing, *Endurance*, 69

"What this means to us": Lees diary, Nov. 4, 1915

"She's going!": Lees diary, Nov. 21, 1915

"I cannot write about it": quoted in Alexander, *The* Endurance, 109

Chapter 8: A Miserable Job

Lees added sausage: incident described in Lees diary, Nov. 22, 1915. Lees spends a lot of time complaining to his diary that no one but him understands the need to ration their food.

"nasal trombone": Worsley diary, March 12, 1916

"As far as I have seen": quoted in Lansing, *Endurance*, 89

"I hate to see so much good food": Lees diary, Dec. 22, 1915

"The Boss at any rate has changed his mind": Wordie, "Weddell Sea Log," Dec. 29, 1915

"His sublime optimism": quoted in Butler, *The* Endurance

Chapter 9: Lash Up and Stow!

"Lees and Worsley are the only pessimistic ones": quoted in Lansing, *Endurance*, 108

"The result was very satisfactory": Hurley diary, Feb. 19, 1916

"stewed penguin heart": McNish diary, Feb. 17, 1916

"The monotony of life here": quoted in Lansing, *Endurance*, 104

"At times like this": quoted in Lansing, *Endurance*, 118

"Hunger is now our lot": Lees diary, March 24, 1916

"We implore him not to get thin": quoted in Lansing, *Endurance*, 122

"Land in sight!": Lees diary, March 23, 1916

"General rejoicing!": Hurley diary, March 23, 1916

"A flock of Dominican gulls passed over": Lees diary, March 24, 1916

"[W]e are in the hands of a Higher Power": quoted in Lansing, *Endurance*, 135

Chapter 10: An Infinity of Ice

"Are you alright?": Shackleton, *South*, 121

"infinity of ice-covered ocean-berg fragments": Hurley diary, April 11, 1916

"splitting, pulverising crash": Lees diary, April 11, 1916

"Never was dawn more anxiously awaited": Hurley diary, April 13, 1916

"wild and savage": Hurley diary, April 15, 1916

"misers gloating over hoarded gold": Shackleton, *South*, 140

Chapter 11: Our Only Hope

"How delicious to wake": Hurley diary, April 15, 1916

"like the courtyard of a prison": quoted in Smith, *Sir James Wordie*, 81

"A more inhospitable place": quoted in Lansing, *Endurance*, 185

"dragged from their bags": Wordie, "Weddell Sea Log," April 21, 1916

"I don't think there will be many survivors": McNish diary, April 20, 1916

"The boss is wonderful": quoted in Alexander, *The Endurance*, 130

"I would rather die": Lees diary, April 23, 1916

"six proven veterans": Hurley diary, April 24, 1916

"She is our only hope": Wordie, "Weddell Sea Log," April 25, 1916

Chapter 12: Across the Sea

Their first night out in the *Caird:* Worsley recounts Shackleton's reflections that night in Worsley, *Endurance*, 101–105

"One sight . . ." quoted in Lansing, *Endurance*, 226

"that's the last of them": Wild's own account, quoted in
   Alexander, *The* Endurance, 171
"All attempts seemed so hopeless": quoted in Alexander,
   The Endurance, 173
He figured they'd made 128 miles: distances and the account
   of the Caird's journey are from Shackleton, *South*, 152–191;
   Worsley, *Endurance*, 101–123; and Worsley's notes in his
   diary, probably made shortly after the boat journey
"This is the first time we have seen it": Lees diary, May 2, 1916
"We manage to get most of our gear": Worsley diary,
   May 4, 1916
"the most motley and unkempt assembly": Hurley diary,
   May 10, 1916

Chapter 13: Over the Mountains

The men picked their way across the foot of a glacier:
   crossing of South Georgia described in this account
   taken mostly from Shackleton, *South*, 192–204, and
   Worsley, *Endurance*, 145–162
"Starboard!" "Port!" "Steady!": Worsley, *Endurance*, 148
"Lash up and stow!": Shackleton, *South*, 215
"Installing ourselves for the winter": Hurley diary,
   May 23, 1916
"In spite of everything": quoted in Lansing, *Endurance*, 202

"It's not good to do that kind of thing": Worsley, *Endurance*, 156

"Don't you know me?": Shackleton, *South*, 201

Chapter 14: Last Stand

They steamed out of the bay and turned west for Elephant Island: account of the rescue attempts based on Shackleton, *South*, 205–217, and Worsley, *Endurance*, 163–179

"Rejoice to hear of your safe arrival": Shackleton, *South*, 209

"One cannot help but be a bit anxious": Lees diary, June 7, 1916

"without even so much as thinking": quoted in Lansing, Endurance, 209

"Everyone spent the day rotting": quoted in Alexander, *The* Endurance, 176

"The idea of a ship ever coming now": Lees diary, Aug. 29, 1916

"Wild, there's a ship!": Lees diary, Aug. 30, 1916

"Are you all well?": Worsley, *Endurance*, 179

Epilogue: Coming Home

"I had to say goodbye": quoted in Alexander, *The* Endurance, 188

"We were like men arisen from the dead": Shackleton, *South*, 205

"'E ought ter 'ave been at the war": quoted in Alexander, *The* Endurance, 188

"Tripp, you don't know what I've been through": quoted by Fergus Fleming in the introduction to Shackleton, *South*, xii

"I am just good as an explorer": quoted in Smith, *Shackleton*, 271

"Shackleton afloat was a more likeable character": quoted in Smith, *Shackleton*, 399

"a pair of excitable kids": quoted in Huntford, *Shackleton*, 689

"Ah what memories": quoted in Alexander, *The Endurance*, 194

"I shall go on going": quoted in Huntford, *Shackleton*, 689

ACKNOWLEDGMENTS

I owe a great debt to a couple of writers who spent years researching the *Endurance* expedition. Shane Murphy and Margot Morrell put in long hours transcribing diaries from the crew members, most of which are unpublished and housed in research libraries from England to Australia to New Zealand. Shane was generous enough to share them with me. Rob Stephenson, who coordinates an informal group of researchers called the Antarctic Circle, also saved me many hours by pointing me in fruitful directions.

I'm grateful to Marc Aronson for the series title and to Marc and John Glenn for helping to shape the idea. Many thanks also to friends and colleagues Leda Schubert, Daphne Kalmar, Lauren Tarshis, Rick Vanden Bergh, Jeff Fannon, and John Hollar.

Laura Williams McCaffrey gave the book its first expert read and reality check. Elizabeth Ward answered a last-minute plea for help. Richard Olson read with care and insight, and Jill Olson trudged gamely through the ice. Writing can be a lonely craft, and the gift of time and interest from friends, colleagues, and family is indispensable.

Thanks as always to Miriam Altshuler for her wise advice and for truly caring about the books. Thanks to Paige Hazzan, who is moving on to an adventure of her own, to Amanda Shih for picking up where Paige left off, and to Lisa Sandell for taking the series under her wing.

And finally, I'm eternally grateful to Estie and Richard for giving me whatever survival skills I possess; and to Jill, Zoë, and Finn for surviving me.

ABOUT THE AUTHOR

TOD OLSON is the author of the historical fiction series How to Get Rich and the first three books in this series, *Lost in the Pacific, 1942*; *Lost in Outer Space*; and *Lost in the Amazon*. He holds an MFA from Vermont College of Fine Arts and lives in Vermont with his family, his mountain bike, and his electric reclining chair.

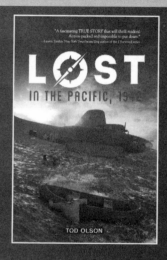
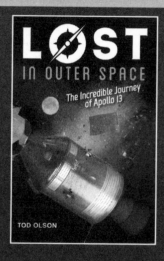
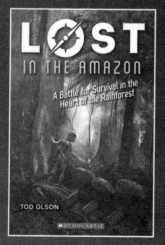
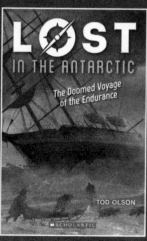